TAPESTRY

WORD
STRAND 1

TAPESTRY

The **Tapestry** program of language
materials is based on the concepts
presented in *The Tapestry of
Language Learning: The Individual
in the Communicative Classroom* by
Robin C. Scarcella &
Rebecca L. Oxford.

Each title in this program focuses on:

Individual learner strategies and
instruction

The relatedness of skills

Ongoing self-assessment

Authentic material as input

Theme-based learning linked to task-
based instruction

Attention to all aspects of
communicative competence

WORD STRAND 1

Meredith Pike-Baky

Laurie Blass

Heinle & Heinle Publishers
An International Thomson
Publishing Company
Boston, Massachusetts, 02116, USA

ITP

The publication of *Word Strand 1* was directed by the members of the
Heinle & Heinle Global Innovations Publishing Team:

David C. Lee, Editorial Director
John F. McHugh, Market Development Director
Lisa J. McLaughlin, Senior Production Services Coordinator

Also participating in the publication of this program were:

Director of Production: Elizabeth Holthaus
Publisher: Stanley J. Galek
Senior Assistant Editor: Kenneth Mattsson
Production Editor: Maryellen Eschmann Killeen
Manufacturing Coordinator: Mary Beth Hennebury
Full Service Project Manager/Compositor: PC&F, Inc.
Art: Dave Blanchette and PC&F, Inc.
Interior Design: Maureen Lauran
Cover Design: Maureen Lauran
Photo/Video Specialist: Jonathan Stark

02735

Copyright © 1996 by Heinle & Heinle Publishers

Manufactured in the United States of America

ISBN: 0-8384-6068-2

Heinle & Heinle Publishers is an International Thomson Publishing Company.

10 9 8 7 6 5 4 3 2 1

Dedicated to the memory of
Juan Freudenthal

PHOTO CREDITS

WELCOME TO TAPESTRY

*E*nter the world of Tapestry! Language learning can be seen as an ever-developing tapestry woven with many threads and colors. The elements of the tapestry are related to different language skills like listening and speaking, reading and writing; the characteristics of the teachers; the desires, needs, and backgrounds of the students; and the general second language development process. When all these elements are working together harmoniously, the result is a colorful, continuously growing tapestry of language competence of which the student and the teacher can be proud.

This volume is part of the Tapestry Program for students of English as a second language (ESL) at levels from beginning to "bridge" (which follows the advanced level and prepares students to enter regular postsecondary programs along with native English speakers). Upper level materials in the Tapestry Program are also appropriate for developmental English courses—especially reading and composition courses. Tapestry levels include:

Beginning	Advanced
Low Intermediate	High Advanced
High Intermediate	Bridge

Because the Tapestry Program provides a unified theoretical and pedagogical foundation for all its components, you can optimally use all the Tapestry student books in a coordinated fashion as an entire curriculum of materials. (They will be published from 1993 to 1996 with further editions likely thereafter.) Alternatively, you can decide to use just certain Tapestry volumes, depending on your specific needs.

Tapestry is primarily designed for ESL students at postsecondary institutions in North America. Some want to learn ESL for academic or career advancement, others for social and personal reasons. Tapestry builds directly on all these motivations. Tapestry stimulates learners to do their best. It enables learners to use English naturally and to develop fluency as well as accuracy.

Tapestry Principles

The following principles underlie the instruction provided in all of the components of the Tapestry Program.

EMPOWERING LEARNERS

Language learners in Tapestry classrooms are active and increasingly responsible for developing their English language skills and related cultural abilities. This self direction leads to better, more rapid learning. Some cultures virtually train their students to be passive in the classroom, but Tapestry weans them from passivity by providing exceptionally high interest materials, colorful and motivating activities, personalized self-reflection tasks, peer tutoring and other forms of cooperative learning, and powerful learning strategies to boost self direction in learning.

The empowerment of learners creates refreshing new roles for teachers, too. The teacher serves as facilitator, co-communicator, diagnostician, guide, and helper. Teachers are set free to be more creative at the same time their students become more autonomous learners.

HELPING STUDENTS IMPROVE THEIR LEARNING STRATEGIES

Learning strategies are the behaviors or steps an individual uses to enhance his or her learning. Examples are taking notes, practicing, finding a conversation partner, analyzing words, using background knowledge, and controlling anxiety. Hundreds of such strategies have been identified. Successful language learners use language learning strategies that are most effective for them given their particular learning style, and they put them together smoothly to fit the needs of a given language task. On the other hand, the learning strategies of less successful learners are a desperate grab-bag of ill-matched techniques.

All learners need to know a wide range of learning strategies. All learners need systematic practice in choosing and applying strategies that are relevant for various learning needs. Tapestry is one of the only ESL programs that overtly weaves a comprehensive set of learning strategies into language activities in all its volumes. These learning strategies are arranged in eight broad categories throughout the Tapestry books:

Forming Concepts
Personalizing
Remembering New Material
Managing Your Learning
Understanding and Using Emotions
Overcoming Limitations
Testing Hypotheses
Learning with Others

The most useful strategies are sometimes repeated and flagged with a note, "It Works! Learning Strategy . . ." to remind students to use a learning strategy they have already encountered. This recycling reinforces the value of learning strategies and provides greater practice.

RECOGNIZING AND HANDLING LEARNING STYLES EFFECTIVELY

Learners have different learning styles (for instance, visual, auditory, hands-on; reflective, impulsive; analytic, global; extroverted, introverted; closure-oriented, open). Particularly in an ESL setting, where students come from vastly different cultural backgrounds, learning styles differences abound and can cause "style conflicts."

Unlike most language instruction materials, Tapestry provides exciting activities specifically tailored to the needs of students with a large range of learning styles. You can use any Tapestry volume with the confidence that the activities and materials are intentionally geared for many different styles. Insights from the latest educational and psychological research undergird this style-nourishing variety.

OFFERING AUTHENTIC, MEANINGFUL COMMUNICATION

Students need to encounter language that provides authentic, meaningful communication. They must be involved in real-life communication tasks that cause them to *want* and *need* to read, write, speak, and listen to English. Moreover, the tasks—to be most effective— must be arranged around themes relevant to learners.

Themes like family relationships, survival in the educational system, personal health, friendships in a new country, political changes, and protection of the environment are all valuable to ESL learners. Tapestry focuses on topics like these. In every Tapestry volume, you will see specific content drawn from very broad areas such as home life, science and technology, business, humanities, social sciences, global issues, and multiculturalism. All the themes are real and important, and they are fashioned into language tasks that students enjoy.

At the advanced level, Tapestry also includes special books each focused on a single broad theme. For instance, there are two books on business English, two on English for science and technology, and two on academic communication and study skills.

UNDERSTANDING AND VALUING DIFFERENT CULTURES

Many ESL books and programs focus completely on the "new" culture, that is, the culture which the students are entering. The implicit message is that ESL students should just learn about this target culture, and there is no need to understand their own culture better or to find out about the cultures of their international classmates. To some ESL students, this makes them feel their own culture is not valued in the new country.

Tapestry is designed to provide a clear and understandable entry into North American culture. Nevertheless, the Tapestry Program values *all* the cultures found in the ESL classroom. Tapestry students have constant opportunities to become "culturally fluent" in North American culture while they are learning English, but they also have the chance to think about the cultures of their classmates and even understand their home culture from different perspectives.

INTEGRATING THE LANGUAGE SKILLS

Communication in a language is not restricted to one skill or another. ESL students are typically expected to learn (to a greater or lesser degree) all four language skills: reading, writing, speaking, and listening. They are also expected to develop strong grammatical competence, as well as becoming socioculturally sensitive and knowing what to do when they encounter a "language barrier."

Research shows that multi-skill learning is more effective than isolated-skill learning, because related activities in several skills provide reinforcement and refresh the learner's memory. Therefore, Tapestry integrates all the skills. A given Tapestry volume might highlight one skill, such as reading, but all other skills are also included to support and strengthen overall language development.

However, many intensive ESL programs are divided into classes labeled according to one skill (Reading Comprehension Class) or at most two skills (Listening/Speaking Class or Oral Communication Class). The volumes in the Tapestry Program can easily be used to fit this traditional format, because each volume clearly identifies its highlighted or central skill(s).

Grammar is interwoven into all Tapestry volumes. However, there is also a separate reference book for students, *The Tapestry Grammar,* and a Grammar Strand composed of grammar "work-out" books at each of the levels in the Tapestry Program.

Other Features of the Tapestry Program

PILOT SITES

It is not enough to provide volumes full of appealing tasks and beautiful pictures. Users deserve to know that the materials have been pilot-tested. In many ESL series, pilot testing takes place at only a few sites or even just in the classroom of the author. In contrast, Heinle & Heinle Publishers have developed a network of Tapestry Pilot Test Sites throughout North America. At this time, there are approximately 40 such sites, although the number grows weekly. These sites try out the materials and provide suggestions for revisions. They are all actively engaged in making Tapestry the best program possible.

AN OVERALL GUIDEBOOK

To offer coherence to the entire Tapestry Program and especially to offer support for teachers who want to understand the principles and practice of Tapestry, we have written a book entitled, *The Tapestry of Language Learning. The Individual in the Communicative Classroom* (Scarcella and Oxford, published in 1992 by Heinle & Heinle).

A Last Word

We are pleased to welcome you to Tapestry! We use the Tapestry principles every day, and we hope these principles—and all the books in the Tapestry Program—provide you the same strength, confidence, and joy that they give us. We look forward to comments from both teachers and students who use any part of the Tapestry Program.

Rebecca L. Oxford
University of Alabama
Tuscaloosa, Alabama

Robin C. Scarcella
University of California at Irvine
Irvine, California

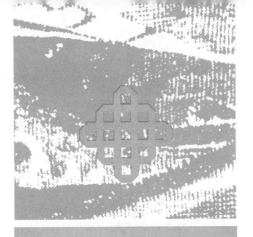

PREFACE

Word Strand 1 is a vocabulary program designed to address the needs of students in high-beginning English as a Second Language classes. It is appropriate for adult and intensive programs at secondary through university levels. *Word Strand 1* can serve as the core text for a vocabulary class or as a supplemental activity text for a reading, oral communication, or multi-skills course. Instructors can teach chapters in any order according to the interests of the students, course syllabus, or current issues and topics; or they can move through the chapters sequentially and take advantage of recycling activities in each.

We feel strongly that any vocabulary-building program at the high-beginning level works best if:

- context is the departure point for learning a *set* of words that respond to a particular theme, task, setting, or situation
- the context is real and dynamic
- the context offers opportunities for students to connect text material to their immediate lives
- students are able to *interact* with the text by labeling word lists, writing captions for photos, and adding some of their own relevant material
- students see the same words in similar and different contexts
- students work in various configurations (individually, in pairs, triads, small groups, and teams) to complete tasks
- students have regular opportunities to reflect on their learning and assess their progress
- the content is fresh and lively, so it is fun to study and fun to teach

Word Strand 1 radiates from five umbrella concepts that suggest useful themes and meaningful contexts for high-beginning students of English as a Second Language. These are Places, People, Food, Fun, and Tools. In turn, each theme generates two chapters that provide opportunities for students to learn new words and review and recycle old words. For example, Chapter 1 is *Places: Where Are You From?* In this chapter, students talk about their countries and languages of origin. Chapter 2 is *Places: How's the Weather?* Here, students use place names to talk about climate. In this way, students increase their ability to communicate about related topics.

How *Word Strand 1* Is Organized

A typical *Word Strand 1* chapter has the following sequence:

PART 1: WORDS IN CONTEXT

This section begins by presenting the chapter's key vocabulary and concepts through art and authentic reading passages accompanied by brainstorming and analysis activities. These activities build confidence by requiring students to draw upon prior knowledge as they explore new material. The section winds up with the Word Bank, a listing of all the new words in the chapter. Each Word Bank is followed by a series of questions that elicit useful facts about the items—rules associated with spelling, pronunciation, semantics, and syntax. This activity not only helps students learn the meaning but the form and use of new words.

PART 2: WORD EXTENSIONS

Word Extensions include activities that help students generate additional lexical items based on those presented in Part 1. These activities teach students how to extend their vocabularies on their own by generating synonyms, antonyms, and creating new forms through the use of affixes. When appropriate, this section also includes activities that present and practice rules of structure and usage particular to some of the vocabulary items.

PART 3: USING WORDS

This section lets students use the vocabulary presented in the chapter in a variety of creative and authentic speaking and writing activities. These activities:

- promote critical thinking skills
- help students personalize concepts
- allow students to synthesize material from the current and previous chapters and put it to use in new, real-life situations

The section also includes one or more word games. These games direct the students to work in teams in order to reinforce new vocabulary.

PART 4: ASSESSMENT

The Assessment section has two components. The first part allows students to review and test themselves on chapter material. The second part is student-centered: it enables students to assess their learning in terms of their own needs, and extend the learning experience by setting personal goals. Students can look forward to this opportunity in every chapter.

Acknowledgments

We gratefully acknowledge the support and inspiration of Dave Lee, Ken Mattsson, Rebecca Oxford, and Robin Scarcella. In addition, we would like to thank the following reviewers, whose comments were invaluable in the shaping of this book:

Susana Christie, San Diego State University;

Lee Culner, Miami-Dade Community College;

Debra Dean, University of Akron;

Marta Dmytrenko-Ahrabian, Wayne State University;

John Fitzer, State University of New York at Buffalo;

Keith Folse, Mobile, Alabama;

Guillermo Perez, Miami-Dade Community College;

Elizabeth Templeman, University College of the Cariboo; and

Mary Wood, Kansas State University.

To the Student

Welcome to *Word Strand 1!* With help from this book, your classmates, and your teacher, you will develop your vocabulary, build your confidence, and increase your fluency in English. Before you begin, we would like to give you a few tips:

- Start a Word Journal. A Word Journal is a notebook just for words. In it, write down each new word you learn. Give each group of new words a title. For example, the first group of new words you will see in Chapter 1 is Areas. Use word group titles from the book or think of your own. In each word group, organize the new words into lists that will help you. You might choose to list words according to parts of speech: Nouns, Verbs, Adjectives, etc. Or you might group words according to what you have trouble with: Words That Are Hard to Spell, Words That Are Hard to Remember, etc.
- Practice using your new words often. Try them out when you talk to your friends and classmates. Review your Word Journal.
- When a native speaker uses a new word you've never heard before, ask him or her what it means. Then write it in your Word Journal.

Finally, we would like to know how this book works for you and what words you add to it. Send us a letter c/o Heinle & Heinle, 20 Park Plaza, Boston, MA. 02116. You can also contact us by e-mail at tapestry@heinle.com.

Meredith Pike-Baky and Laurie Blass

CONTENTS

Places: Where Are You From?

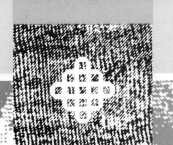

GEOGRAPHICAL AREAS OF THE WORLD

People like to talk about where they come from. In this chapter, you'll find many words that answer the question: "Where are you from?"

PART 1: WORDS IN CONTEXT

Take a Look

These students are introducing themselves on the first day of class. Read what they say. Note each student's name, and where he or she is from.

My name is Sotirios.
I'm from Greece.

My name is Isabel, and
I'm from El Salvador.
El Salvador is in Central
America.

I'm Luis. I'm from Brazil.
I speak Portuguese.

My name is Akiko.
I'm from Japan.

My name is Kin Yee.
I'm from Taiwan.

Now read the list again. This time, match the student's name with the country he or she comes from.

Akiko	Taiwan
Kin Yee	Japan
Sotirios	El Salvador
Isabel	Greece
Luis	Brazil

Read About It

Read the information in the following table. It shows where some recent immigrants to the United States came from.

LEARNING STRATEGY

Forming Concepts: Putting new words into context helps you understand them more fully.

Where do most recent immigrants to the United States come from?					
Latin America and the Caribbean	44%	Middle East	4%	Africa	3%
Asia	29%	Eastern Europe	4%	India	4%

Adapted from *Time* magazine, Fall 1993.

Check Your Understanding

Threads

There's no place
like home.

Dorothy, *The Wizard of Oz*

1. Label the world map. Write the areas from the list below in the correct locations on the map.

   North America   Caribbean   Middle East   Africa
   Latin America   Asia   Eastern Europe   India

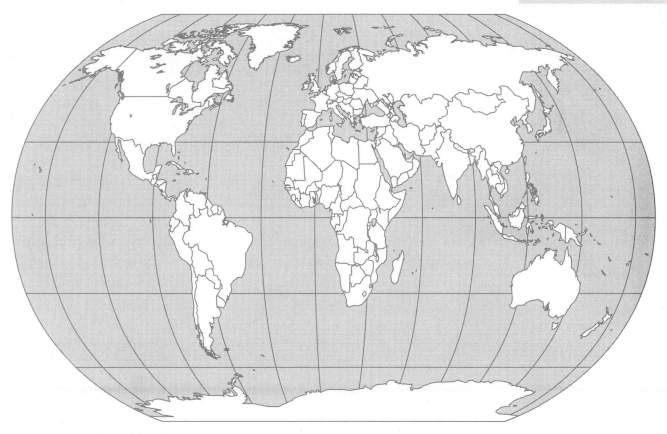

2. Now use the table above to answer these questions with a partner:
   a Where do most immigrants to the United States come from?
   b. Where do the fewest immigrants to the United States come from?
   c. What percent of immigrants to the United States come from Asia?
   d. Where do most immigrants to your native country come from?

Forming Concepts: Putting new words into context helps you understand them more fully.

Word Bank

New words for this chapter are organized into four groups: Areas, Countries, People, and More Nouns. Write these words and any other new words in your Word Journal.

AREAS

North America	Latin America	the Caribbean
Europe	Eastern Europe	the Middle East
Asia	Southeast Asia	Africa
Central America		

Add your own area names:

_____ _____ _____ _____

_____ _____ _____ _____

Overcoming Limitations: Knowing important facts about new words lets you use them immediately with confidence.

Questions
1. What word must you use with both of these place names: *Caribbean* and *Middle East?*
2. Why are Eastern and Southeast capitalized in *Eastern Europe* and *Southeast Asia?*

Answers
2. When compass directions (*north, south, east, west, southeastern,* etc.) are part of geographical place names, they are always capitalized.
1. You must use *the* before Caribbean and Middle East.

COUNTRIES

Iran	Ethiopia	Poland	Canada	Haiti
Brazil	Ghana	Egypt	Mexico	China
Japan	Jamaica	Lebanon	Korea	Cambodia
El Salvador	India	Greece	Italy	Russia

Add your own area names:

_____ _____ _____ _____

_____ _____ _____ _____

Which country names in English are similar to or the same as country names in your native language?

PEOPLE

Iranian	Ethiopian	Canadian	Haitian	Brazilian
Ghanaian	Egyptian	Mexican	Chinese	Japanese
Jamaican	Lebanese	Korean	Cambodian	El Salvadorian
Greek	Italian	Indian	Pole	Russian

Add your names for people:

_____   _____   _____   _____

_____   _____   _____   _____

Questions
1. What word ending do most of the names for people have?
2. What word ending do the names for people from Japan, Lebanon, and China have?
3. The people from the country of India are called "Indians." What do we call natives of North America?

Answers

1. Most of the names of people from these countries end in *-n, -an,* or *-i/ean.* (Exceptions: People from Poland are *Poles* and people from Greece are *Greeks.*)
2. The names of people from Japan, Lebanon, and China all end in *-ese.*
3. Natives of North America are *Native Americans.*

MORE NOUNS

immigrant   import   product   native language/country   location

PART 2: WORD EXTENSIONS

Prepositions with Places: in

When you talk about the country where you live, or where a country is located, you use <u>in</u>.

EXAMPLES   I live <u>in</u> Canada
Canada is <u>in</u> North America.

Practice using <u>in</u> to talk about location. First, draw a line to match the country with its area. Then make sentences with <u>in</u> to describe the location.

EXAMPLE   Ghana is <u>in</u> Africa.

Country	Area
Canada	Africa
Brazil	Latin America
Haiti	Asia
Poland	Southeast Asia
Iran	the Middle East
China	the Caribbean
Ghana	North America
Cambodia	Eastern Europe

Word Forms: Adjectives

When you talk about a thing or a person from a country, you use the adjective form
of the country name. For example, for people or things from France, you can say:

> I have a <u>French</u> car.
> The <u>French</u> make great cars.
> There's a <u>French</u> woman in my class.

Notice that you can say either *the French* or *the French people* when you're
talking about the people in general, as a group. But you must follow the adjective
form (French) with a noun (woman) when you're talking about a specific person.

Practice identifying these adjective forms. First, draw a line to match the
country name with the correct adjective.

Country	Adjective
Brazil	Italian
China	Indian
Mexico	Canadian
Haiti	Egyptian
Egypt	Brazilian
India	Chinese
Canada	Mexican
Italy	Haitian

Now, rewrite these phrases. Change the country name to an adjective. Follow
the example.

1. a product from <u>France</u> *a French product*

2. an import from <u>Japan</u> _____

3. a fan from <u>China</u> _____

4. a book from <u>Egypt</u> _____

5. a car from <u>Italy</u> _____

6. a woman from <u>Canada</u> _____

Word Forms: Countries to Languages

Country names are sometimes related to language names, but not always.

EXAMPLE	Country		Language
	Japan	—>	Japanese
		but	
	Brazil	—>	Portuguese

Work in small groups and fill in the language names for each country in the
following chart.

NOTE Some countries have more than one language, and not all languages
are listed.

Language Names

French	Hindi	Chinese
English	Portuguese	Farsi
Arabic	Spanish	

LEARNING STRATEGY

Forming Concepts: Putting words into categories helps you use them in new situations.

COUNTRY	LANGUAGES(S)
Canada	*English French*
Brazil	
Mexico	
China	
Haiti	
Iran	
Egypt	

Threads

The top 10 foreign languages spoken in the United States: Spanish, German, Italian, French, Polish, Yiddish, Swedish, Norwegian, Greek, and Czech.

The Ethnic Almanac

PART 3: USING WORDS

Use Words Creatively

LEARNING STRATEGY

Personalizing: Using new words to talk about yourself helps you remember them.

1. In small groups, talk about your home country. Talk about:
   • what part of the world it is in
   • what languages are spoken there
   • where most immigrants to your country come from
2. Work in small groups. Choose one person to take notes (the note taker), and one person to report on your group's answers (the reporter). Answer these questions:
   • Where do some imports in your country come from? What are they?
   • What do you like/dislike about them?
3. Write a paragraph about one of the following:
   • Yourself: Where are you from? What is your native language?
   • Your native country: Where is it? Who lives there? (Where do most immigrants come from?) What languages do people speak?

Threads

Most people in Ireland speak English, but some speak Irish, or *Gaeltacht*.

Word Game

WHERE IS IT?

Work with a partner. Complete this map of the world. Your map (Map A) has some of the countries on the list filled in. Your partner's (Map B) has some of the others filled in. Some countries are not filled in on either map. Complete your map by listening to your partner's clues.

LEARNING STRATEGY

Remembering New Material: *Playing* with new words makes remembering them easy.

Countries

Iran	Ethiopia	Poland	Canada	Haiti
Brazil	Ghana	Egypt	Mexico	China
Japan	Jamaica	Lebanon	Korea	Cambodia
El Salvador	India	Greece	Italy	Russia

EXAMPLE   Student A: Where is Korea?
Student B: It's in Asia. It's near Japan.
Student A: Where is Japan?

MAP A

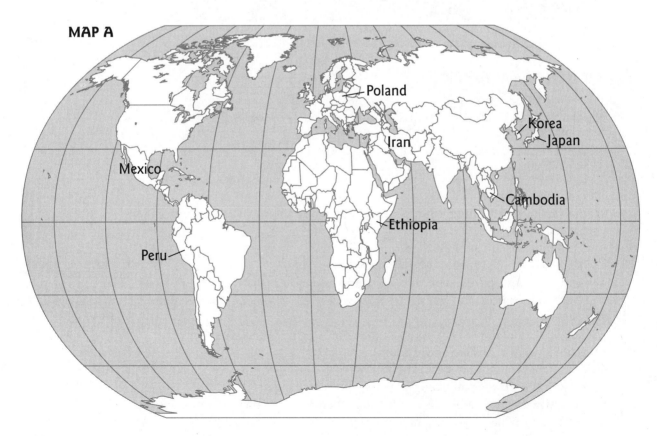

MAP B

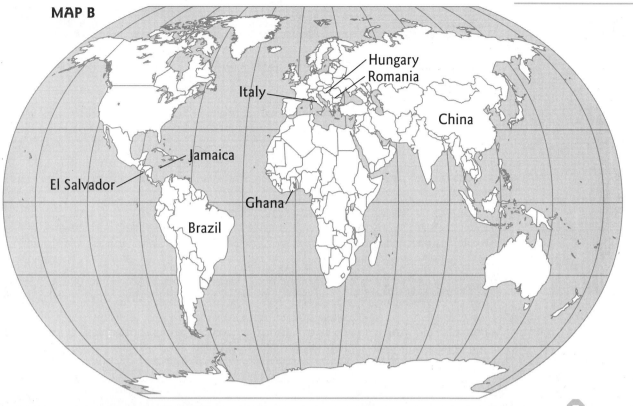

Hungary
Romania
Italy
China
Jamaica
El Salvador
Ghana
Brazil

PART 4: ASSESSMENT

Review

Work in small groups. Review area and country names with the following activity: Student A says a country or area name. Student B says a country name that starts with the last letter of Student A's country name.

EXAMPLE Eastern Europe—> Ethiopia—> Asia—> etc.

Test Yourself

Test your knowledge of the meanings of the words in this chapter. Fill in the blanks with the correct forms of the words.

1. A person from Lebanon is _____.
2. A person from El Salvador is _____.
3. A person from Canada speaks either ____ or ____ or both.
4. Two countries in Asia are _____ and _____.
5. Poland is in _____.
6. If you are from Greece, you might speak _____.
7. A car from Italy is _____.
8. Egypt is in _____.
9. A person from _____ may speak _____.
10. Two countries in _____ are _____ and _____.

Look Back

What did you learn about words for areas, countries, people, and languages around the world?

_____

_____

_____

_____

_____

_____

Look Ahead

What else do you want to learn about words for areas, countries, people, and languages around the world? How will you do this?

_____

_____

_____

_____

_____

_____

Places: How's the Weather?

2

INTERNATIONAL WEATHER

People like to talk about the weather. They also like to complain about it! In this chapter, you'll discover many weather words and expressions.

PART 1: WORDS IN CONTEXT

Take a Look

Look at these photos of places around the world. Describe them. What do you see? What's the weather like? Would you like to live there? Work in small groups and write some words to describe the photos.

_____
_____
_____
_____
_____

_____
_____
_____
_____
_____

_____
_____
_____
_____
_____

LEARNING STRATEGY

Forming Concepts: Brainstorming for new words makes you more fluent.

Read About It

Look at the following weather map for the United States. Read the forecast and *pretend* you already understand any new words.

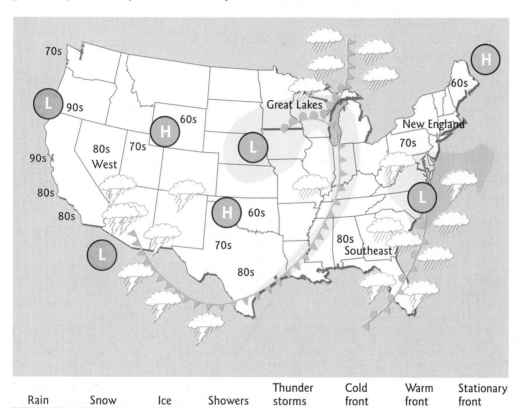

Rain	Snow	Ice	Showers	Thunder storms	Cold front	Warm front	Stationary front

NATIONAL FORECAST:

There will be heavy rain and thunderstorms in parts of the Southeast and the mid-Atlantic states today as tropical storm Wendell enters the region. To the north, a storm system will cause scattered showers across the Great Lakes. The West will have sunny, warm, and dry weather conditions, but the Southwest will have afternoon thundershowers.

LEARNING STRATEGY

Overcoming Limitations: Guessing the meaning of new words increases your reading fluency.

Check Your Understanding

Check your understanding of the forecast and the map by doing the following activities. Work in small groups.

1. Look at the passage titled "National Forecast," and underline all the words that describe **regions** in the United States.
2. Now, circle all the words in the paragraph that describe **weather.**
3. Look again at the weather map and the key below it. Put your finger on each of the following.
   - a region that has showers
   - a region that has thunderstorms
   - a region that has rain
4. Does any region on the map have snow?
5. Does any region have ice?

	U.S. TEMPERATURES					U.S. TEMPERATURES					U.S. TEMPERATURES			
	Yesterday Lo/Hi	Today Lo/Hi	Sky	Tomorrow Lo/Hi	Sky		Yesterday Lo/Hi	Today Lo/Hi	Sky	Tomorrow Lo/Hi	Sky		Yesterday Lo/Hi	Today Lo/Hi	Sky	Tomorrow Lo/Hi	Sky

City	Yesterday Lo/Hi	Today Lo/Hi	Sky	Tomorrow Lo/Hi	Sky
Albany NY	44/80	47/74	CL	49/67	CY
Albuquerque	55/81	50/73	PC	45/75	PC
Amarillo	62/80	46/66	CL	43/73	CL
Anchorage	44/56	42/55	PC	40/54	PC
Asheville	50/72	52/72	CY	52/73	PC
Atlanta	64/75	60/79	PC	62/78	PC
Atlantic City	46/75	57/67	CY	62/68	RN
Baltimore	53/78	57/70	CY	63/69	RN
Birmingham	56/80	59/82	PC	63/78	RN
Bismarck	49/60	37/59	PC	37/70	CL
Boise	45/86	46/79	CL	48/83	CL
Boston	58/78	58/69	CY	55/65	CY
Brownsville	65/90	67/94	PC	66/90	PC
Buffalo	53/80	55/77	CL	57/71	PC
Burlington VT	50/79	50/75	CL	49/73	CY
Casper	33/41	26/63	CL	31/70	CL
Charleston SC	68/72	63/76	CY	65/79	PC
Charleston WV	49/79	52/79	PC	60/75	PC
Charlotte NC	59/76	60/74	RN	61/77	CY
Cheyenne	30/54	27/55	PC	35/59	PC
Chicago	57/82	61/75	RN	55/67	CY
Cincinnati	53/81	53/77	PC	57/75	PC
Cleveland	54/79	55/78	PC	57/76	PC
Colorado Springs	39/67	37/60	CL	35/61	PC
Columbia SC	64/78	62/75	CY	61/82	PC
Columbus OH	51/80	52/77	PC	54/77	PC
Concord NH	42/82	43/70	CL	43/67	CY
Dallas-Ft Wroth	63/88	64/74	CY	50/76	PC
Denver	33/65	38/64	CL	36/66	CL
Des Moines	59/86	56/60	RN	47/62	CY

Yesterday's high and low temperatures for 24 hours ending 5 P.M. Pacific time.

City	Yesterday Lo/Hi	Today Lo/Hi	Sky	Tomorrow Lo/Hi	Sky
Detroit	58/81	58/80	CL	58/79	CL
Duluth	57/72	53/59	RN	50/58	CY
El Paso	72/82	63/88	PC	57/86	PC
Fairbanks	28/60	34/53	PC	35/48	PC
Fargo	51/59	43/56	PC	43/67	PC
Flagstaff	42/66	39/70	CL	37/70	CL
Great Falls	35/58	35/70	CL	45/80	CL
Hartford	47/81	52/74	CY	53/68	CY
Helene	43/63	30/70	CL	36/78	CL
Honolulu	77/91	77/90	CL	77/90	CL
Houston	59/89	63/89	PC	60/80	PC
Indianapolis	56/83	56/79	PC	57/72	CY
Jackson Miss	59/82	61/86	PC	63/77	PC
Juneau	49/56	50/56	RN	49/56	RN
Kansas City	64/73	53/58	CY	44/58	CY
Las Vegas	65/91	66/93	PC	63/93	PC
Lincoln	51/83	48/55	RN	39/58	RN
Little Rock	64/83	63/78	RN	54/69	PC
Los Angeles	62/81	64/84	PC	65/83	PC
Louisville	55/83	58/79	PC	61/75	CY
Medford	51/101	54/100	CL	53/96	CL
Memphis	61/83	64/82	CY	63/72	CY
Miami Beach	74/87	74/88	RN	75/89	PC
Milwaukee	65/82	62/71	CY	61/68	CY
Mpls-St Paul	60/80	56/61	RN	53/59	RN
Mobile	63/84	65/85	PC	65/80	CY
Montgomery	60/85	61/85	PC	63/83	CY
Nashville	58/81	58/82	PC	62/72	CY
New Orleans	72/86	66/88	PC	66/83	CY
New York City	59/81	62/73	PC	61/67	RN
Newark	58/83	63/74	PC	62/68	RN
Oklahoma City	58/87	52/68	RN	45/69	PC
Omaha	57/82	49/55	RN	40/58	RN

City	Yesterday Lo/Hi	Today Lo/Hi	Sky	Tomorrow Lo/Hi	Sky
Orlando	70/84	70/88	PC	70/88	PC
Philadelphia	56/79	59/71	CY	63/69	RN
Phoenix	71/82	75/94	CY	74/96	PC
Pittsburgh	50/79	51/77	PC	55/74	CY
Portland ME	48/76	50/66	CL	46/64	CY
Portland OR	57/90	57/89	CL	56/85	CL
Providence	51/79	54/69	CY	54/67	CY
Raleigh	55/72	59/69	RN	59/74	CY
Rapid City	41/56	32/58	PC	36/69	CL
Reno	49/85	47/85	CL	49/85	PC
Richmond	52/75	60/70	RN	62/72	RN
St Louis	63/83	64/70	RN	53/62	CY
Salt Lake City	53/80	47/76	CL	47/80	CL
San Antonio	61/90	65/89	CY	57/84	CL
San Diego	66/75	66/75	PC	66/75	PC
San Francisco	56/68	56/69	PC	56/72	PC
Santa Fe	50/78	45/68	PC	37/70	PC
Seattle	59/81	55/85	CL	55/76	CL
Shreveport	60/89	65/86	CY	58/80	PC
Sioux Falls	49/78	48/55	RN	43/62	RN
Spokane	52/75	45/79	CL	48/82	CL
Tampa-St Pete	71/88	71/88	PC	71/89	PC
Tucson	69/86	67/93	CY	66/95	PC
Tulsa	61/84	57/64	CY	45/59	CY
Washington	58/77	59/72	CY	63/70	RN
Wichita	63/83	51/64	PC	44/58	CY
Yakima	48/83	46/85	CL	45/85	CL
Yuma	72/88	75/97	CY	76/98	PC

NATION'S HIGH AND LOW

Death Valley, CA	Stanley, ID
106°	23°

INTERNATIONAL Yesterday's low and high temperatures and sky conditions for 24 hours ending 5 P.M. Pacific time

■ CANADA				■ CARIBBEAN				■ EUROPE				■ AFRICA/MIDEAST				Manila	77/86	PC
Calgary	28/54	CL		Barbados	73/86	RN		Amsterdam	50/63	DZ		Algiers	57/90	CL		Seoul	60/77	PC
Edmonton	31/60	CL		Havana	75/89	CY		Copenhagen	50/61	PC		Cairo	75/95	CL		Singapore	79/92	RN
Ottawa	50/78	PC		Nassau	72/89	RN		Dublin	50/60	PC		Kuwait	78/101	CL		Tokyo	71/81	CY
Toronto	49/80	CL		San Juan	74/88	CY		Lisbon	58/68	PC		■ ASIA				■ PACIFIC		
■ MEXICO				■ LATIN AMERICA				London	48/68	RN		Bangkok	81/94	CY		Fiji	70/82	PC
Acapulco	72/96	RN		Bogota	43/72	CY		Paris	45/62	PC		Bombay	71/86	PC		Melbourne	43/54	PC
La Paz	76/99	CY		Caracus	73/91	CY		Rome	58/76	RN		Delhi	71/93	CL		Sydney	50/56	PC
Mexico City	54/74	PC		Lima	61/68	CY		Warsaw	51/56	RN		Hong Kong	79/85	RN		Tahiti	78/81	RN

CL	= clear	CY	= cloudy	PC	= partly cloudy	RN	= rain
SN	= snow	FG	= fog	IC	= ice	DZ	= drizzle
WN	= wind	M	= missiing				

6. Now look at the key below the temperature tables and answer these questions: What does CL mean? What does PC mean? RN?

> **NOTE** To tell a temperature, use *degrees*. For example: "It was 78 degrees in Boise yesterday." The symbol ° means *degree(s)*.

7. In the U.S. table, what was the high temperature in New York City? What was the low temperature in Spokane? What was the high temperature in Bogota?

8. Find the city you're in now, or one near you, in the tables. What was the high temperature? The low?

Word Bank

Here are the new words found in this chapter. Add them to your Word Journal.

WEATHER WORDS

rain	(thunder)storm	cloud	humid	tropical
fog	breeze	wind	arid	climate
snow	a front	lightning	wet	cool
ice	hot	warm	smog	forecast
showers	cold	sun	dry	

Question

❶ What's the noun form for *humid?* For *hot?*

Answer

❶ *Humid* (adjective), *humidity* (noun); *hot* (adjective), *heat* (noun)

MORE WEATHER WORDS

region	high/low pressure	light	Fahrenheit
clear	heavy	unsettled	Celsius
drizzle	conditions	temperature	degree
haze	mist		

Questions

❷ Name one country that measures temperatures in *Fahrenheit,* and one that uses *Celsius.*

❸ Give examples of some *regions* in the United States, and name some states or cities in each region you think of.

❹ What word from the "More Weather Words" list means about the same thing as "a light rain?"

Answers

❹ Another word for "a light rain" is a *drizzle. Drizzle* is also a verb.

❸ Some names for regions in the United States come from compass directions, e.g., the West, the Southwest, the East, the South, the Northeast, etc. Some regions come from geographical features: the Great Lakes, the (Pacific/Atlantic) coast, the mid-Atlantic, the Gulf, etc. Examples of states and cities: the west—California; the southwest—Arizona, New Mexico; the mid-Atlantic—New York City; the Great Lakes—Michigan; the Gulf—Texas.

❷ The United States measures temperatures in Fahrenheit. France measures them in Celsius. Can you think of other examples?

THE EFFECTS OF WEATHER

| nervous | crazy | strange | depressed | irritable |
| happy | energetic | sad | blue | cranky |

**Forming Concepts: Comparing the meanings of new words helps
you understand them better.**

Questions
○ Which two words in "The Effects of Weather" are similar in meaning to
sad?
○ Which word means the same as *irritable?*

Answers

⑥ *Cranky* means the same as *irritable*, but it's less formal.

⑤ *Blue* and *depressed* are similar to *sad. Blue* is less formal than *sad* and
depressed.

Now, add any other weather words you know:

_____ _____ _____ _____

_____ _____ _____ _____

PART 2: WORD EXTENSIONS

Word Forms: Nouns to Adjectives

Threads

A noun is a person,
place, or thing.

Many nouns have adjective forms. Follow these rules when changing nouns to
adjectives:

• For nouns ending in more than one vowel and a consonant (like *rain*), just
add *-y* (*rainy*)
• For one-syllable nouns ending in one vowel and a consonant (like *smog*),
double the last consonant and add *-y* (*smoggy*).
• For nouns that end in vowel-consonant-e (*ice*), drop the final *-e* and add *-y*
(*icy*).

Give the adjective forms of these weather nouns:

rain _____   wind _____

snow _____   fog _____

ice _____   breeze _____

sun _____   smog _____

cloud _____

Makes Me Feel . . .

One way to talk about the effects of weather is to talk about how it makes us feel. Take a look at these sentences:

> Rainy weather <u>makes me feel</u> blue.
> Cool weather <u>makes me feel</u> energetic.
> An arid wind <u>makes some people feel</u> crazy.

Complete these sentences about how certain types of weather make you feel:

1. Rainy weather makes me feel _____.

2. Cool weather makes me feel _____.

3. A hot sun makes me feel _____.

4. Humidity makes me feel _____.

5. A dry wind makes me feel _____.

6. Cloudy skies make me feel _____.

Threads

The world's coldest city:
Ulan-Bator, Mongolia.
Average temperature:
24.8 F (–4.0 C)

The People's Almanac

PART 3: USING WORDS

Use Words Creatively

1. Many languages have proverbs, sayings, and jokes about the weather and how people feel about it.

    EXAMPLE   A saying about the foggy weather in San Francisco is: "The coldest winter I ever spent was a summer in San Francisco."

LEARNING STRATEGY

Managing Your Learning: Sharing information with others gives you more opportunities for learning.

In small groups, share information about what people in your country or culture think and say about the weather. Share:

• proverbs or sayings about the weather
• jokes about the weather
• quotations about the weather from famous writings or authors

LEARNING STRATEGY

Personalizing: Using new words to talk about how the weather makes *you* feel helps you understand their meanings.

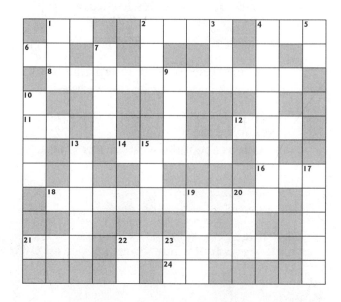

2. Work in small groups. Talk about how the weather makes you feel. Choose one person to take notes (the note taker), and one person to report on your group's answers (the reporter). Answer these questions:

- How do you feel when it rains?
- How do you feel when it's sunny?
- How do you feel when it is very cold? Very hot?
- What weather conditions make you feel strange or uncomfortable?

When you finish discussing, have the reporter tell your group's answers to the class.

3. Write a paragraph about one of the following:

- What's your favorite kind of weather? Why?
- Explain a proverb, saying, or joke about the weather in your language, or in any language.
- You are thinking about moving to a new place. How important will climate be in your decision?

Word Game

CROSSWORD PUZZLE

Work with a partner to complete the crossword puzzle. Use the following words and clues.

Clues

Across

1. The abbreviation for *high temperature* on a weather map.
2. This is frozen, and it falls from the sky.
4. This is very thick mist.
6. _____ the north, a storm system will cause scattered showers.
8. "78 degrees" is a _____.
11. People often feel cheerful _____ a sunny day.
12. When it snows, the roads can become _____.
14. When there is a strong breeze, it is _____.
16. This is a planet and it gives off heat.
18. This scale is used to measure temperatures in the U.S.
21. This is another word for *arid*.
22. This is a light rain.
24. You might find this abbreviation for *northeast* on a weather map.

Down

1. When the weather's like this, take off your coat.
2. On a clear day, you can _____ very far.
3. It is generally _____ during the rainy season.
4. This is the name for a prediction about the weather.
5. People often _____ to tropical places for their vacation.
7. This is a name for air polution. It increases with warm weather.
9. Weather that falls from the sky.
10. The weather can be _____ when there is a breeze.
13. If there is a _____ storm, people cannot go outside.
15. This is the opposite direction from *south*.
19. This is often caused by smog and warm weather.
20. Humid weather can make some people feel this way.
23. Some people prefer to live _____ cold climates because they like to see the seasons change.

Word List

heavy	go	ill
icy	north	snow
windy	smog	forecast
NE	dry	rain
wet	ice	in
drizzle	Fahrenheit	fog
see	hi	haze
sun	to	hot
on	cool	temperature

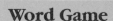

Recycle

Do the following activity in small groups. Combine words from this chapter with words from Chapter 1.

Pretend you are a tour guide. Tell a group of tourists about the weather in different countries around the world.

Optional: Write your answer to the Recycle activity.

PART 4: ASSESSMENT

Review

Review the words that describe weather and its effects by playing a game. Work in teams. Give examples of places in the world that have the following weather conditions. Work quickly. The first team to finish with all correct answers wins.

1. A place where it is very arid:

_____

2. A place where it is very humid:

_____

3. A place where there is snow on the ground all year round:

_____

4. A place that has an arid wind that affects the feelings and behavior of people:

_____

5. A place famous for being foggy:

_____

6. A place other than the United States that uses the Fahrenheit temperature scale:

_____

7. A big city in a tropical region:

_____

8. A city outside the United States that is very smoggy:

_____

9. A city that has warm weather during December, January, and February:

_____

10. A place that often has tropical storms:

_____

Test Yourself

Test your knowledge of the meanings of words in this chapter by selecting the correct words from the list to complete the sentences that follow.

climate	warm	hot	nervous	cool
tropical	snowy	arid	smog	regions

I have lived in many _____ in the United States, and I've
$\quad$ 1
known a lot of different weather conditions. I grew up in the Southeast, and

we often had _____ storms. These came at the end of
$\quad$ 2

summer when it was very _____ and the wet air was
$\quad$ 3

humid. I thought they were scary—thunderstorms still make me feel

_____ .
$\quad$ 4

When I grew up, I moved to California. I went to college in Los Angeles, a

city famous for its _____ . However, many long-time residents
$\quad$ 5

say the air is cleaner nowadays than it was before. Los Angeles is pretty

_____ year-round, and in the fall, a hot, _____ wind
$\quad$ 6 $\qquad\qquad\qquad$ 7

blows from the desert and makes people irritable.

Now I live in New England. It has the best _____ for me. In
$\quad$ 8

the spring and fall the air is _____ and refreshing, and the
$\quad$ 9

winters are cold and _____ . The summers are hot, but at least
$\quad$ 10

there are no tropical storms!

Look Back

What did you learn about words that describe weather and how it makes people feel?

_____

_____

Look Ahead

What else do you want to learn about words about weather? How do you plan to do this?

_____

_____

People: What Do They Do?

3

PEOPLE AND PROFESSIONS

When we talk about people, we often are interested in what they do or where they work. In Chapter 3, you'll discover a variety of words and expressions for describing people's jobs and professions.

PART 1: WORDS IN CONTEXT

Take a Look

Look at these people. They graduated from college ten years ago. What are they doing today? What are their occupations? Work in small groups and write your guesses next to each photo.

Northern University
Class of 1988
What Are They Doing Today?

Sandy Greenbaum

She's _____.

She's a(n) _____.

Yolanda Gutierrez

She's _____.

She's a(n) _____.

Manny Madriaga

He's _____.

He's a(n) _____.

Overcoming Limitations: Making guesses makes you more fluent and more confident.

Read About It

Read the information in the following table. It shows the fastest growing occupations in the United States from 1986 to 2000.

FASTEST GROWING OCCUPATIONS 1986–2000 (Numbers in thousands)		
OCCUPATION	EMPLOMENT 1986	Projected 2000
Salespersons, retail	3,579	4,780
General managers and top executives	2,383	2,965
Truck drivers	2,211	2,736
Accountants	945	1,322
Computer programmers	479	813
Food preparation workers	949	1,273
Teachers, kindergarten, and elementary	1,527	1,826
Receptionists and information clerks	682	964
Computer systems analysts	331	582
Licensed practical nurses	631	869
Electrical and electronics engineers	401	592
Lawyers	527	718

Bureau of Labor Statistics, Occupational Outlook Quarterly, Spring 1988.

Check Your Understanding

1. Which of these are the fastest growing occupations, according to the table: electrical and electronics engineers, salespersons, computer programmers?

2. Which occupations have something to do with computers?

3. Which occupations have something to do with food?

4. For which occupations do you need a college degree?

5. For which occupations do you probably need good communication skills?

6. For which occupations do you probably need to be strong?

24

LEARNING STRATEGY

Forming Concepts: Analyzing what you've read helps you better understand new information.

Now, match the occupations on the left with the job responsibilities—the things you do on a job—on the right. There may be more than one responsibility for each job.

Occupation

lawyer
elementary school teacher
computer systems analyst
corporate manager
accountant
receptionist
restaurant cook
salesperson
electrical engineer

Responsibilities (Things You Do on a Job)

plans lessons
draws blueprints
designs homes and buildings
designs computer systems
advises companies on how to manage money
prepares food to order
helps customers select purchases
operates a cash register
designs electrical systems
assigns jobs or tasks to corporate employees
plans project schedules
designs curriculum
teaches reading skills
advises companies on how the law affects
    their businesses
advises people accused of crimes

LEARNING STRATEGY

Forming Concepts: Associating new information with what you already know increases your knowledge.

Word Bank

Here are the new words for this chapter. They are organized into three groups: People, Things, and Actions. Add them to your Word Journal.

PEOPLE

lawyer
computer systems analyst
accountant
restaurant cook
electrical engineer

elementary school teacher
corporate manager
receptionist
salesperson
architect

Threads

Average starting salary at a large law firm in 1992: $75,000.

The American Almanac of Jobs and Salaries

Questions

① Which words end with *-s* in the plural form?

② Which word has an irregular plural? That is, which word changes its form to make it plural? What is its plural form?

Answers

① All the words end in *-s* in the plural form except salesperson.

② Salesperson becomes salespeople in the plural form.

LEARNING STRATEGY

Remembering New Material: Putting new information into categories helps you remember it better.

THINGS

electrical system	computer system
project schedule	curriculum
occupation	employment
responsibility	blueprint
cash register	profession

Questions

③ Which words are countable? Which one is noncountable?

④ Which word has an irregular plural?

Answers

③ All the words are countable except *employment*.

④ The plural form of *curriculum* is *curricula*.

ACTIONS

plan	design
advise	prepare
draw	operate
assign	require

Questions

⑤ These action words are verbs. Which two verbs can you also use as nouns in the same form that you see here?

⑥ Which of these verbs have an irregular past form?

Answers

⑤ You can use *plan* and *design* as nouns, e.g., "José Luis has a good *plan*." "Akiko worked on her *design* all day."

⑥ *Draw* is *drew* in its past form.

Word Associations

You can increase your vocabulary if you think about all the additional words a single word suggests. Word associations also help you remember word meanings. Here's how you do it: Just take a cue word, for example *draw*, and say or write all the words it makes you think of: paint, picture, create, design, plan, etc.

Now try this with the following words from the Word Bank. Use these guidelines to make associations: Think of words that are

- similar to the cue word in meaning or form
- examples of the cue word
- in the same category as the cue word

draw: _____

profession: _____

employment: _____

teacher: _____

manager: _____

cook: _____

Word Forms

Many job titles are related to verbs that describe what people do and the fields in which they work. Look at the examples, and then finish the chart with the correct verbs and field names that go with each job title. Notice that:

- some verb expressions are *practice* + noun. For example: "to practice law."
- some job titles have related field words, but no related verb. (When you see "X," it means "No related form.") For example, for Job Title *engineer*, there's the Field *engineering*, but there is no verb.

JOB TITLE (Person)	VERB	FIELD
teacher	*to teach*	*teaching*
programmer		
manager		
engineer		
cook		
salesperson **HINT** Don't use *person* in the related word forms.		
lawyer	*to practice law*	*law*
accountant		
architect	*to design*	

26

Use Words Creatively

1. In small groups, discuss your answers to these questions:

   • What profession do you want to have?
   • Why do you want to have this profession?

   One person in the group will be the recorder—he or she will take notes—and one will be the reporter.

   When you are finished, have the reporter tell your group's answers to the class.

Threads

There were 1,354,000 employed engineers in the United States in 1992.

Occupational Outlook Handbook 1994–1995. U.S. Department of Labor

LEARNING STRATEGY

Personalizing: Giving personal examples for new words helps you remember the new words and understand them more fully.

2. Write a paragraph about one of the following:

   • A profession you want, and why you want it.
   • A person you know who has one of the jobs in this chapter.
   • An unusual job you know of.

Word Game

TWENTY QUESTIONS

Play Twenty Questions with a partner. To play, Student A thinks of an occupation. Student B asks only "Yes" or "No" questions until he or she guesses the answer.

EXAMPLE   Do you use a computer in your work?
            Do you work with food? Etc.

LEARNING STRATEGY

Overcoming Limitations: Playing word games increases your confidence.

Recycle

Do at least one of the following activities in small groups. Combine words from this chapter with words from previous chapters.

1. Pretend you're at a party. You don't know any of the other people at the party. Introduce yourself and talk about where you are from, what you do, and what the weather is like today.
2. A classmate wants to move to your native country. Tell him or her about the best jobs in your country. Explain why.
3. Pretend you are a job counselor—someone who helps people choose the best job for them. Explain to a group of job-seekers how weather affects certain professions.

   Optional: Write your answers to the Recycle activities.

PART 4: ASSESSMENT

Review

Review the meanings of words in the Word Bank by matching the items on the left with the definitions on the right.

1. _____ to make a plan for something such as a picture, a building, a computer system, etc.

2. _____ a person who advises people about the law

3. _____ someone who helps customers make purchases

4. _____ a person who instructs others or helps them acquire a skill

5. _____ the plans that an architect draws when designing a house or building

6. _____ a place people go to be served food that they order from a menu

7. _____ a person who prepares food

8. _____ someone who designs bridges, machines, computer systems, etc.

9. _____ a description of what students will study at a particular level or in a particular course

10. _____ a person who advises people and companies on how to manage their money

a. an engineer
b. an accountant
c. a lawyer
d. a cook
e. a teacher
f. curriculum
g. to design
h. a clerk
i. restaurant
j. blueprint

Test Yourself

Test your knowledge of the meanings of the words presented in this chapter by taking the following quiz. Circle the letter before the word or phrase that best completes the sentence.

1. An accountant
   a. prepares food to order.
   b. advises people accused of crimes.
   c. advises companies on how to manage money.

2. A systems analyst
   a. teaches reading skills.
   b. designs computer systems.
   c. advises companies on how the law affects their business.

3. A person who designs homes and buildings is
   a. an architect.
   b. a lawyer.
   c. a restaurant cook.

4. A person who designs machines, bridges, or electrical systems is
   a. a receptionist.
   b. an elementary school teacher.
   c. an engineer.

5. A corporate manager
   a. plans lessons.
   b. draws blueprints.
   c. assigns jobs or tasks to employees.

6. Another word for *occupation* is
   a. responsibility.
   b. profession.
   c. project.

7. A teacher
   a. designs curriculum.
   b. helps customers select purchases.
   c. designs homes and buildings.

8. An architect uses _____ in his or her work.
   a. a cash register
   b. blueprints
   c. a curriculum

9. A landscape architect designs
   a. gardens.
   b. schools.
   c. concert halls.

10. A software engineer works with
    a. machines.
    b. airplanes.
    c. computers.

Threads

Year the first computer was used in business: 1954, at J. Lyons & Co., London.

Look Back

What did you learn about words for people and professions in this chapter?

_____

_____

_____

_____

Look Ahead

What else do you want to learn about words for people and professions? How do you plan to do this?

_____

_____

_____

_____

People: What's This Person Like?

We like to talk about people. We often wonder: Is he nice? Is she funny? Are they smart? In this chapter, you'll look at ways to describe people.

PART 1: WORDS IN CONTEXT

Take a Look

Look at these pictures of people. Then read what their friends say about them:

Kati

Let me tell you about Kati: I like her because she's funny; she's always telling jokes and doing funny things. Once, she played a trick on our teacher . . .

Ping

Ping's my best friend. She's very dependable. She always helps me when I need to talk to someone.

Paolo

I like Paolo. We work together. He's great to work with because he's so intelligent. He always finds solutions to problems at work. He finds ways to do things faster or to make more money for the company.

Rick

Rick is very thoughtful. Once, when I was sick, he brought me soup and magazines. I was also absent a lot, and he helped me do my schoolwork.

Read the descriptions again. This time, write one word that describes each person:

1. Kati: _____   **3.** Paolo: _____

2. Ping: _____   **4.** Rick: _____

Read About It

Read the following excerpts from job advertisements in the newspaper. Guess the meaning of any words you don't know.

Administrative Assistant—Berkeley engineering company needs well-organized, efficient assistant for general office work. Must have Mac experience and be reliable and self-motivated. Send resume to IDA, 555 Blake Street, Berkeley, CA 92100.

Office Manager—Wanted: Bright, energetic, flexible person to work pt in small, fast-paced office. Must have experience and references. Send resume to Admin., 609 Bush St., SF, CA 90002.

Computer Project Manager—New West Bank is looking for an ambitious, talented individual to join its Product Management Group. Send resume to: New West Bank, 65478 Market Street, SF, CA 90002.

LEARNING STRATEGY

Overcoming Limitations: Guessing the meaning of new words helps you read faster and builds your confidence.

Check Your Understanding

With a partner, answer these questions about the ads.

1. Which job is for a bank?

   _____

2. Which job is for an engineering company?

   _____

3. What kind of office is the "Office Manager" position for?

   _____

4. Match the following abbreviations from the ads to the words they probably stand for:

   SF   Administration
   St.   Macintosh (computer)
   Admin.   San Francisco
   pt   Street
   Mac   part time

5. Underline the adjectives in each ad that describe someone's personality.

Word Bank

Here are the new words for this chapter. Add them to your Word Journal.

WORDS THAT DESCRIBE PEOPLE

funny	dependable	intelligent	thoughtful
flexible	efficient	reliable	self-motivated
bright	energetic	independent	ambitious
talented	responsible	friendly	helpful
kind	nice	sensitive	strong
outgoing	warm	generous	well-organized
fast-paced	references	individual	salary

Questions

- Which adjectives end in *-able* or *-ible*?
- Which end in *-ed*?
- Which end in *-ent*?
- What word in the list means almost the same thing as *kind*? What means the same thing as *bright*? What other synonyms can you find in the list?

Answers

1. *Responsible, dependable, flexible, reliable*—These adjectives come from nouns that end in *-ability* or *-ibility: responsibility, dependability,* etc.
2. *Talented, self-motivated, well-organized*—Except for *talented,* these come from verbs that end in silent *-e: to motivate, to organize.*
3. *Intelligent, efficient, independent*—These come from nouns that end in *-ence: independence, intelligence,* etc. Notice that *efficient* is different; it comes from *efficiency.*
4. *Kind = thoughtful; bright = intelligent.*

PART 2: WORD EXTENSIONS

Synonyms

Thinking of synonyms for words you already know increases your vocabulary. Work with a partner. Study the words in the following list. Then read the words in the Word Wheels. Write words in the spokes that mean about the same thing. Add words of your own. Look at the example before you start.

dependable	intelligent	thoughtful
self-motivated	bright	responsible
friendly	nice	outgoing
warm	generous	

Word Wheels

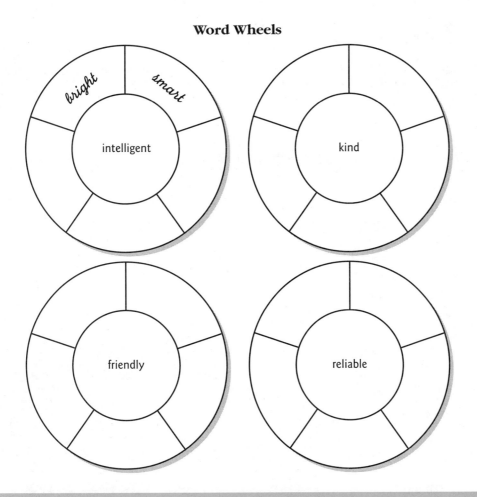

Antonyms

You can make opposites from some of the words in the Word Bank by putting *un-*, *in-*, or *ir-* in front of them.

   Match the following words with those in the antonym boxes. Put the word with the opposite meaning in the correct box. Be sure that both words are the same form.

inefficient   unintelligent   irresponsible
insensitive   untalented   unfriendly
thoughtless   undependable   inflexible

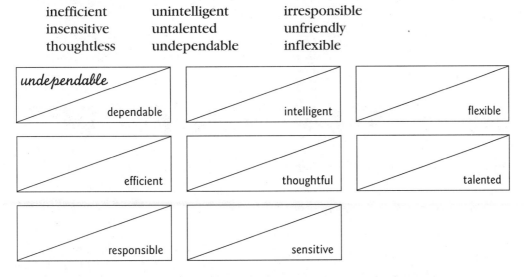

Now, give an example of each opposite you wrote in the boxes.

EXAMPLE   *irresponsible————> someone who loses things you lend him or her*

36

LEARNING STRATEGY

Remembering New Material: Giving examples for new words helps you remember them.

Word Forms: Adjectives to Nouns

In Word Bank, Part 1, you saw that many personality adjectives come from nouns.

> ***EXAMPLE*** One of Paolo's qualities is <u>intelligence</u>; he's <u>intelligent</u>.
>   noun   adjective
>
> He's an <u>intelligent</u> person.
>   adjective

Work with a partner. Fill in Column B. Use the nouns from the list that are related to the adjectives in Column A.

Threads

If you want to lift yourself up, lift up someone else.

Booker T. Washington
in *And I Quote*

sensitivity

generosity

ambition

energy

efficiency

reliability

independence

intelligence

warmth

talent

responsibility

flexibility

dependability

A ADJECTIVES	B NOUNS
flexible	
talented	
dependable	
efficient	
energetic	
responsible	
warm	
reliable	
independent	
sensitive	
generous	
ambitious	

Comparatives and Superlatives

When you compare two people's qualities you either

- add *-er* to the adjective.

  EXAMPLE Juan is *nicer* than Pablo.

  Or

- use *more* in front of the adjective.

  EXAMPLE Juan is *more dependable* than Pablo.

When you describe the most extreme example of a quality, you

- add *-est* to the adjective.

    EXAMPLE Juan is the *nicest* man I know.

    Or

- use *most* in front of the adjective.

    EXAMPLE Juan is the *most dependable* man I know.

Generalizations:

For one-syllable words (*warm, nice*) and two-syllable words ending in *-y* (*busy, friendly*),

- add *er* or *est.*

For other two-syllable words and three-or-more-syllable words,

- use *more* or *most.*

Work with a partner and write in the comparative and superlative forms of each of the adjectives from the Word Bank.

ADJECTIVE	COMPARATIVE	SUPERLATIVE
funny		
dependable		
intelligent		
thoughtful		
flexible		
efficient		
reliable		
self-motivated		
bright		
energetic		
independent		
ambitious		
talented		
responsible		
friendly		
helpful		
kind		
nice		
sensitive		
strong		
out-going		
warm		
generous		
*well-organized		
*This one's tricky!!		

Use Words Creatively

LEARNING STRATEGY

Forming Concepts: Using new words to describe people you know helps you understand both the forms and the meanings of the words.

1. In small groups, talk about people you know: family members, friends, neighbors, classmates, teachers. You can use either of the following patterns:

X is _____ (adjective).

EXAMPLE   Stéphane is *experienced*.

Or

X is a/an ____ (adjective) + ____ (noun).

EXAMPLE   Stéphane is an experienced pilot.

LEARNING STRATEGY

Managing Your Learning: Giving examples helps you think clearly about an idea, and it also helps other people understand you better.

Also, it's a good idea to give examples when you describe personality characteristics, as the people did in Part 1, Take a Look, on page 32.

EXAMPLE   Stéphane is an experienced pilot; he's flown across the Atlantic many times.

Use the adjectives from this chapter, including their synonyms and antonyms.

NOTE   You can use words like *very* and *extremely* in front of the adjectives you want to emphasize.

LEARNING STRATEGY

Forming Concepts: Comparing two things helps you better understand both of them.

2. Compare famous people using the comparative forms of adjectives.

EXAMPLE   Charlie Chaplin was funnier than the Marx Brothers.

3. Write a paragraph about the funniest, smartest, meanest, or most _____ person you've ever known. Give several examples. Trade paragraphs with a partner. Read your partner's paragraph and answer this question:
  • Do you have a clear picture of the person your partner is describing? Why? Why not? If not, make suggestions for more adjectives and/or examples.

Overcoming Limitations: Role playing in a comfortable place—your classroom—makes speaking in the real world easier.

4. Role-play a job interview. One student is the employer; the other is the job seeker. The employer asks the job seeker to describe the qualities he or she has that would make him or her right for the job. You and your partner can choose any job you want. Then trade roles.
5. Write an advertisement for your ideal:
  • husband/wife   • classmate   • co-worker
  • teacher   • boss   • child

Word Game

WORD SCRAMBLE

Unscramble the following words from the Word Bank:

visnestei   _____

cien   _____

gingtuoo   _____

marw   _____

nikd   _____

gronts   _____

Threads

Children are the wisdom of the nation.

West African saying
in *And I Quote*

Recycle

Do at least one of the following activities in small groups. Combine words from this chapter with words from previous chapters.

1. You have two friends who don't know each other. You want them to meet. Describe Friend A to Friend B, and Friend B to Friend A. Say where each one is from, what he or she does, and what he or she is like.
2. You own a large, international business. You are looking for employees for different jobs around the world. Give a group of job seekers the following information:
  • what jobs are available   • what the weather is like in those places
  • where they are located   • what kind of person you want for each job

Optional: Write your answers to the Recycle activities.

Review

Give an example to match each adjective.

| Adjective: funny | Example: tells jokes |
| intelligent | got all As last term |

Adjective	**Example**
flexible	_____
dependable	_____
energetic	_____
responsible	_____
independent	_____
sensitive	_____
generous	_____
ambitious	_____

Test Yourself

Test your knowledge of the meanings of the words presented in this chapter by taking the following quiz. First, read the letter. Then, fill in the blanks with words from this list.

| efficient | dependable | friendly | talents | reliable |
| intelligent | responsible | generous | warmth | warm |

Dear Mrs. Sergeant:

I highly recommend Miss Jane Takahashi for the position of office assistant. Jane has worked for me for three years. She is very _____1_____; she always finishes her work on time. She's also _____2_____ ; she understands what to do, and if she doesn't understand, she asks questions.

The customers like Jane because she is very _____3_____ and _____4_____ . Her co-workers like her too, because she's _____5_____ and _____6_____ .

Jane is a special person away from work, too. She has many friends who enjoy her _____7_____ . She's also talented; one of her _____8_____ is playing the piano. She's also _____9_____ ; once a week she helps children learn to read at the neighborhood school.

As I said, I recommend Jane highly. I am sad to see this _____10_____ employee leave.

Sincerely,

Emily Keeler

Emily Keeler

Look Back

What did you learn about words that describe people?

_____

_____

_____

_____

_____

Look Ahead

What else do you want to learn about describing people? How do you plan to do this?

_____

_____

_____

_____

_____

Food: What Do You Eat?

SALADS
GARDEN 2.50
GREEK 3.00
CHEF 3.25

SPECIALTIES
2.95
SOUPS CUP 1.35 BOWL 2.25
FRUIT SALAD PER OZ .22
FROZEN YOGURT PER OZ .22
TOPPINGS PER OZ .22

BREAKFAST CROISSANTS
EGG & CHEESE 1.49
EGG & CHEESE & BACON 1.95
EGG & CHEESE & HAM 1.95

SANDWICHES
HAM & SWISS 2.95
CHICKEN SALAD 2.95
TUNA SALAD 2.95
TUNA MELT 3.25
ROAST BEEF 3.25
B.L.T. 2.25
TURKEY B.L.T. 3.25
CHICKEN PARMESAN 3.50
BOSTONIAN 3.50
ROAST BEEF, HAM TURKEY, CHEESE
DAILY SPECIAL 2.95

ALL SANDWICHES SERVED WITH LETTUCE,
TOMATO , AND PICKLE ON FRENCH BREAD
WHOLE WHEAT, OR CROISSANT.

BAKERY
MUFFINS .70
BAGELS w/CREME CHEESE .90
CINNAMON ROLLS 1.25
COOKIES .90

CROISSANTS
BUTTER .85
CHOCOLATE 1.10
ALMOND 1.15
FRUIT & CHEESE 1.25
STRAWBERRY BLUEBERRY LEMON
HAM & CHEESE 1.90
BACON & CHEDDAR 1.90
SPINACH & FETA 1.90
PIZZA CROISSANT 1.45

5% MEALS TAX NOT INCLUDED

Eating is a pleasure and a necessity of life. That is, we eat because we want to and because we have to. In this chapter you will learn more words to describe the kinds of foods you eat.

LEARNING STRATEGY

Forming Concepts: Taking a class poll gives you new ideas.

Before you begin Chapter 5, talk about something new you have eaten in the last month.

 PART I: WORDS IN CONTEXT

Take A Look

What foods do you eat? Do you eat a lot of one kind of food or a combination of different foods? Study these photos of food and label (give a name for) everything you see. Do this with a classmate, then share your labels with the class.

1. _____

4. _____

2. _____

5. _____

3. _____

6. _____

Read About It

What is good eating? Read the back of a bread package to learn one answer.

A GUIDE TO DAILY FOOD CHOICES
U.S. Dept. of Agriculture

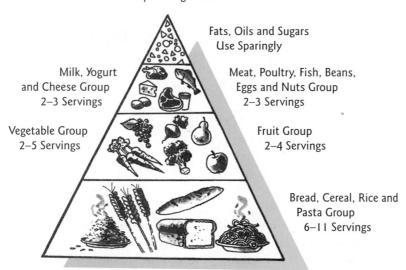

Fats, Oils and Sugars
Use Sparingly

Milk, Yogurt
and Cheese Group
2–3 Servings

Meat, Poultry, Fish, Beans,
Eggs and Nuts Group
2–3 Servings

Vegetable Group
2–5 Servings

Fruit Group
2–4 Servings

Bread, Cereal, Rice and
Pasta Group
6–11 Servings

Check Your Understanding

1. Read the following sentences about the food pyramid and underline the answer that completes the sentence correctly.

   a. The food pyramid comes from _____.
   the bread company   the U.S. Department of Agriculture

   b. You _____ eat the foods at the top of the pyramid often.
   should   shouldn't

   c. You _____ eat the foods at the bottom of the pyramid often.
   should   shouldn't

   d. You should eat more _____ than anything else.
   bread, cereal, rice, pasta   vegetables

   e. Milk and eggs _____ in the same food group.
   are   are not

   f. Pita bread is in the _____ food group.
   bread, cereal, rice, pasta   meat, poultry, fish, beans, eggs, nuts

   g. You should eat fewer _____ than anything else.
   fruits   fats, oils, and sugars

   h. Foods from the bread, cereal, rice, and pasta group are _____.
   high in fat   low in fat

   i. The food pyramid recommends that you eat six to 11 servings from the bread, cereal, rice, and pasta group _____.
   every day   every week

   j. Yogurt and cheese _____ in the same food group.
   are   are not

Remembering New Material: Linking new words with words you already know helps you learn them faster.

2. Now, look at the two columns of words. The meanings of the words on the left are similar to the meanings of the words on the right. Match them by drawing a line between the words that have the same meaning. Use the bread package to help you with new words.

sparingly	the food you eat
guide	portion
serving	chicken
diet	recommendation
poultry	not very much

3. Finally, show that you understand the categories of the food pyramid by writing a specific example of a food for each section. Choose a specific example that is something you have eaten before. Compare your examples with those of your classmates.

FOOD CATEGORY	SPECIFIC EXAMPLE
Fats, Oils, and Sugars	*butter (on toast)*
Milk, Yogurt, and Cheese Group	
Meat, Poultry, Fish, Beans, Eggs, Nuts	
Vegetable Group	
Fruit Group	
Bread, Cereal, Rice, and Pasta Group	

Word Bank

Here are the new words presented in this chapter. Add them to your Word Journal.
Add any new words you've discovered on your own.

FOOD AND EATING

connection	apple
often	asparagus
tradition	beans
foundation	bread
recommend	cereal
sparingly	eggs
nutritious	fats
choices	fish
fresh	fruit
source	ice cream cone
homemade	pears
necessities	potato
pleasures	poultry
energy	steak
servings	sugar
daily	tomato
maintain	vegetables
foods	wheat
flavor	yogurt
ingredients	
diet	
healthy	

Questions

1. The words in the column on the right describe different foods, but they are all the same part of speech. Are these words verbs, nouns, adjectives or adverbs?
2. The words in the column on the left are words you can use when talking or writing about eating. Identify their parts of speech. There are two verbs, 12 nouns, two adverbs, four adjectives, one word that can be both a noun and a verb, and one word that can be both an adjective and an adverb. Work with a partner to complete this as quickly as you can.
3. What are the plural forms of *potato* and *tomato*? How do you spell them and how do you pronounce them?

Answers

3. *potatoes* and *tomatoes* \po·tey·toz\ and \to·mey·toz\
be both an adjective and an adverb.
one word that can be both a noun and a verb (*diet*), and (*daily*) which can
(*often, sparingly*), four adjectives (*nutritious, fresh, homemade, healthy*),
foundation, energy, servings, foods, flavor, ingredients), two adverbs
nouns (*pleasures, necessities, connection, tradition, choices, source,*
2. The words on the left include two verbs (*recommend, maintain*), 12
1. The words on the right are all nouns.

Countable/Noncountable Nouns

When you talk or write about food nouns, you use *a, an* or *the* if the food item is singular and can be counted, or *some, the,* or no article if it is a mass noun and cannot be counted. (You will study countable and noncountable nouns again in Chapter 9.) Study the chart of countable and noncountable food words. Notice that some words (*) can be **both** countable and noncountable. With these words, the noncountable form refers to the general category of the food, and the countable form refers to a specific type or item.

> *EXAMPLES* *I don't like to eat chicken.*
> (Noncountable, referring to any kind of chicken.)
>
> *I am cooking a chicken for dinner tonight.*
> (Countable, referring to one item.)

COUNTABLE	NONCOUNTABLE
egg	asparagus
choice	cheese*
serving	chicken*
ingredient	fish*
food*	fruit*
vegetable	milk
	pasta
	rice
	sugar
	yogurt

LEARNING STRATEGY

Personalizing: Applying your own preferences and experiences to new material will make it more meaningful.

Ask and answer the following questions with a partner to practice using countable and noncountable food words.

1. Some people really like to eat pasta. How many *servings* of pasta can you eat for one meal?
2. Many American children drink milk as they are growing up. Did you drink *milk* as a child?
3. What is your favorite dish? What is an important *ingredient* in that dish?
4. How many kinds of *sugar* have you cooked with or eaten?
5. How many *eggs* do you eat in a week?

Quantifiers with Noncountable Food Words

You can use quantifiers to indicate specific amounts of noncountable food words. For example, if you want to buy some asparagus, you can ask for a **bunch** of asparagus. Or, since you can count quantifiers, you can ask for **two bunches** of asparagus. Study this list of quantifiers:

a basket of
a bowl of
a bunch of
a carton of
a glass of
a kilo of
a quart of
a package of
a plate of
a pound of

_____

_____

_____

_____

1. What other quantifiers have you heard or used? Add these to the list.
2. Now, in a conversation with a classmate, make sentences matching the quantifiers with noncountable nouns.

QUANTIFIERS	NONCOUNT NOUNS
a basket of	asparagus
a bowl of	cheese
a bunch of	fruit
a glass of	chicken
a kilo of	fish
a quart of	milk
a package of	pasta
a plate of	rice
a pound of	sugar
	yogurt
_____	ice cream
_____	
_____	
_____	

Threads

Humans have probably been eating grain for about 6,000 years.

Use Words Creatively

Managing Your Learning: Making lists helps you record ideas quickly.

1. Make a list of everything you ate yesterday. Fill in the empty food pyramid. Then talk to a partner about your eating habits. Do you have a good diet according to the U.S. Department of Agriculture? (See page 45 for an example.) Use your own food pyramid to support your answer when you talk with a classmate.

FOOD I ATE YESTERDAY

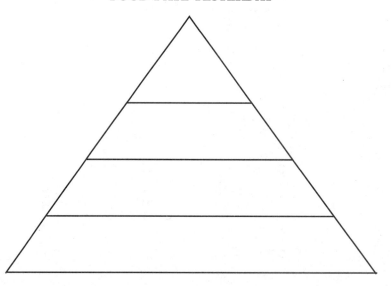

Personalizing: Giving your own interpretation of new material makes it more meaningful.

2. What do you think good eating is? Perhaps you don't agree with the U.S. Department of Agriculture. Make up your own eating recommendations with the kinds of food you think people should eat. You can use a pyramid or a circle, square, or another shape that matches your recommendations.
3. Make one or more food pyramids using food from different cultures. Share each *ethnic food pyramid* with your classmates.

Remembering New Material: Using a basic structure or outline for each theme you encounter aids you in remembering new words.

4. Teach your classmates to make a quick and healthy dish. Use the following format to get you started. Add a drawing and if possible, bring some samples to share.

HOW TO _____

To _____ , use _____

or _____ . Now you're ready to

_____ . Simply _____ and

_____ . _____ can be eaten

_____ . For extra flavor, _____ .

5. Think of a young person you know. Write a short letter to this person, giving advice on the foods he or she should eat to be healthy. Be as specific as you can.

Word Games

STORY CHAIN

Sit in a circle and build a story by recalling what each person ate for breakfast or lunch. Begin like this:

First student: I ate *peanuts* for lunch today.

Second student: I ate peanuts and *a piece of pizza* for lunch today.

Third student: I ate peanuts, a piece of pizza, and *an egg roll* for lunch today.

Play like this for 15 minutes. If you complete the circle and there is time left, begin with lunch yesterday. Try to remember what everyone ate.

If this is too easy, use quantifiers. Another variation of this game is *I Went to the Market.* Practice using vocabulary useful at the grocery store when you play this game.

MAD LIBS

This exercise is similar to a popular word game. In groups of two, help Bill and Lil complete their conversation by filling in words from this chapter. Use the part-of-speech clues to complete the sentences. Check for agreement with articles and plurals. Try to use a different word for each space. Read your conversation to your classmates when you are finished.

BILL   Hey, Lil! I just ate something very strange. It was a _____ .

                                                                         noun

LIL   Wow! Was it _____ ? Was it _____ ?

                                      adjective   *adjective*

BILL   Yes. I don't usually eat _____ , so I found it strange.

                                                noun

LIL   I ate something like that last week. It was _____ and I ate

                                                         noun

        it _____ .

                    adverb

BILL   Why didn't you eat _____ instead?

                                      noun

LIL   Oh, I don't know. I was _____ .

                                        adjective

BILL   Well, I'll never eat _____ again!

                                    noun

LIL   Yes, I agree. You can never _____ a _____

                                      verb   *noun*

        when you do that.

BILL   And, besides, I don't like to eat a lot of _____ .

                                                                        noun

LIL   Neither do I, Bill. Good luck next time you eat something strange!

Recycle

Do at least one of the following activities in small groups. Combine words from this chapter with words from previous chapters.

1. In a casual conversation with your classmates, talk about the connection between the weather in particular areas and the food that is available there. Does the weather determine what you eat? Try to answer this question by giving specific examples.
2. Can you understand a person by knowing the kinds of food she or he eats? Some people believe that people "are what they eat." Pretend that you agree with this by showing how specific people's personalities and styles reflect their eating habits.
3. You are a party planner. People ask you to serve food from all over the world. For your next party you will have seven food tables, each serving food from a different culture or part of the world. Choose the seven types of food you will serve.

Optional: Write your answers to the Recycle activities.

Review

The editor at a food company made some mistakes. Correct the mistakes in the following sentences by replacing the underlined words with vocabulary from this chapter.

1. Sahara Pita Bread uses the finest <u>servings</u> to maintain a tradition of homemade taste and goodness.
2. A healthy diet includes lots of <u>junk food.</u>
3. The food pyramid <u>disagrees with</u> six to 11 servings from the bread group every day.
4. The food pyramid is a <u>monthly</u> guide.
5. Foods from the bread, cereal, rice, and pasta group are an important source of <u>flavor</u>, especially in low fat diets.

Test Yourself

Elena, an exchange student from the Ural Mountains, is living with an American family. Help her write a letter home about the food she eats every day. Choose words from this list to complete the sentences. Use each word once. Check plural forms and articles for clues.

chicken	vegetables	sugar	yogurt
bread	cereal	milk	
pear	fish	apple	

Dear family,

We eat _____ every morning for breakfast. It is very
           1
sweet because it has a lot of _____ in it. I eat it with
                               2
_____. At lunch I have a sandwich with cheese and
      3
_____. I like to eat fruit with my sandwich so I also
      4
eat a _____ or an _____. We often have
           5   6
_____ or steak or _____ for dinner.
      7   8
We always have lots of _____ too. I eat frozen
                              9
_____ for dessert.
      10

53

Look Back

What did you learn about vocabulary for food and eating in this chapter?

_____

_____

_____

_____

Look Ahead

What else do you want to learn about food and eating? How do you plan to do it?

_____

_____

_____

_____

Food: What Do You Drink?

Just as people choose different foods, they also choose different drinks. Some people drink at a certain time of the day, with certain friends, from certain cups or glasses. In this chapter you will study drinking customs around the world.

PART 1: WORDS IN CONTEXT

Take a Look

The people in the following photos are enjoying their favorite drinks. Get together with a partner and look at the photos. Try to guess where they are and what they are drinking. Write your guesses below each picture.

_____

_____

_____

_____

_____

_____

_____

_____

Read About It

Personalizing Your Learning: Sharing your preferences in learning styles and activities with your classmates helps you learn faster.

What do you drink every day? Make a list of your classmates' favorite drinks. Then read the following letter. It was written by Ron, a graduate student and a member of the China-America Friendship Association at his university. He recently traveled to China and sent this letter home.

Dear Family,

I have made many friends in China and have had lots of interesting experiences. I have especially enjoyed tasting new kinds of tea. My favorite part of the day is when I visit a friend because I know we will drink tea. There are two kinds of tea ceremonies in China: formal and informal.

Most of my experiences have been informal, or casual, meetings. Chinese people always serve tea when they have guests. The host makes a full pot of tea and the tea brews in the pot. It could be green tea, black tea or oolong tea. We sit together and talk and drink our tea until we finish the pot.

Yesterday I drank tea at a business meeting. At this formal gathering, we were not served from a teapot. Instead, each of us had our own cup with tea leaves inside. A server poured hot water into everyone's cup and we brewed our own tea in our own cups. We talked about business as we drank. The server refilled the cups with hot water when they became empty.

My favorite tea is Ti Kwan Yin tea. It is a common oolong tea in China, but it is rare in the U.S. It tastes smooth and smells a little like flowers. Tea experts don't drink as much black tea in China as they do in the U.S. For me, drinking tea is an important social custom. It also makes me feel relaxed.

Threads

Tea and coffee make people cheerful and talkative.

Managing Your Learning: Doing exercises by yourself first helps you keep track of your strengths and weaknesses.

Check Your Understanding

1. Work by yourself first. Then check answers with a partner. Circle the correct answer.

   a. Where is Ron?

   China   Chad   India

   b. What is Ron's profession?

   tea grower   businessman   student

   c. Which of the following is **not** true for both formal and informal tea meetings in China?

   people talk   people share a teapot   people drink tea

   d. How many kinds of tea does Ron write about?

   three   four   five

   e. At which kind of meeting do people brew tea in their own teacups?

   casual   formal   informal

   f. How much does Ron like drinking tea?

   not very much   a little   a lot

   g. How does Ron feel when he drinks tea?

   casual   relaxed   formal

   h. What kind of tea is *Ti Kwan Yin?*

   green   oolong   black

2. Make a class chart of drinking habits. Complete the following chart with information from your classmates.

Threads

In France, tisane is served as an after-dinner drink to help people relax.

WHAT YOU DRINK	WHEN YOU DRINK	HOW IT MAKES YOU FEEL

Personalizing Your Learning: Linking another person's experiences to your own makes learning more meaningful.

Word Bank

Here are the new words presented in this chapter. Add them to your Word Journal. Add any new words you've discovered too.

DRINKING CUSTOMS

always	serve
brew	guests
teapot	host
rare	casual
flavor	informal
smooth	formal
smell	pour
aroma	refill
common	

Questions

1. Which word in the Word Bank is a compound word?
2. One of the words contains the sound [z] as in pleasure? Which word is this?
3. The word *flavor* refers to how something tastes. What does *aroma* refer to?
4. Which of these words does *pour* rhyme with: hour, four, flour, door?
5. Which other drinks, besides tea, do you *brew*: orange juice, coffee, cola?
6. Make these words adverbs: *smooth, formal, informal, rare.*
7. Which word means "fill again"?
8. Which word means "not formal"?

Answers

8. *informal*
7. *refill*
6. add -*ly* to all of them: *smoothly, formally, informally, rarely*
5. coffee
4. *four* and *door*
3. the way something smells
2. *casual*
1. *teapot*

Adverbs of Frequency

The following adverbs describe how often you repeat an action or event. Notice that they are listed in order of frequency—from most to least frequent. Study them with a partner, then ask and answer the questions.

always
frequently
often
occasionally
sometimes
once in a while
seldom
rarely
hardly ever
never

How often do you drink Chinese tea?
      drink coffee?
      drink soda?
      drink mineral water?
      drink fruit juice?

      drink _____?

Makes Me Feel . . .

LEARNING STRATEGY

Understanding and Using Emotions: Connecting experiences and feelings helps you remember new words.

People sometimes choose drinks because of the way they make them feel. Study the columns of drinks and feelings then practice making sentences.

DRINKS	FEELINGS
apple juice	nervous
orange soda	happy
coffee	relaxed
tea	sleepy
coke	awake
Dr. Pepper	hot
lemonade	cold
milk	_____
grape juice	_____
water	_____
iced tea	_____
cocoa (hot chocolate)	_____
_____	_____
_____	_____

EXAMPLE *I can't drink coffee at night because it makes me feel nervous.*

Using Words Creatively

Your Limitations: Practicing English with people whom you like and trust helps you gain confidence.

1. Interview a friend outside of class about his or her favorite drinks. Use a chart like you did in class in Part 1 to record your information. Share what you learned with your classmates.

2. Write a letter like Ron's about what you drink every day. Use the following format to get you started. Refer to Word Bank.

Dear _____,

   I have enjoyed _____ in _____.

My favorite part of the day is when _____ because I

know _____.

_____ people always _____.

Yesterday I drank _____ at _____.

At this _____, _____. There were

_____. My favorite _____ is

_____ It is a common _____ in

_____, but it is rare in _____.

It tastes _____ and smells like _____.

I love drinking _____ here. For me, drinking _____

makes me feel _____.

> **Threads**
>
> Iced tea has become a popular summertime drink in the United States.

3. Give a presentation on a common drinking custom in your culture to your classmates. Show pictures and serve the drink if possible.

4. Have a tasting party with your class. Decide on the beverage: tea, coffee, soda, etc. and ask everyone to bring to class one type of the beverage you selected. Number each drink and let everyone taste and rate each drink. Students should vote for the drink they liked best. The drink with the most votes wins.

Word Game

Remembering New Material: Playing a game with words you have just learned will help you remember them.

WHO DRINKS WHAT WHERE?

Divide the class into two teams. Take turns making up sentences about people, drinks, and places. Make sure that the people, drinks, and places begin with the same letter. You can use the same letters again and again but you may not repeat the people, drinks, or places. Give each team a point for each new sentence. The team with the most points at the end wins. Look at these examples:

PEOPLE	DRINKS	PLACES
Donald drinks	**d**iet soda	in **D**enmark.
Maryanne drinks	**m**ilk	in **M**oscow.
Wilhelm drinks	**w**ater	in **W**arsaw.
Susan drinks	**s**aki	in **S**eattle.

Recycle

Do at least one of the following activities in small groups. Combine words from this chapter with words from previous chapters.

1. In an informal conversation with your classmates, talk about the relationship between what you drink and the weather. Which drinks make you feel warm? Which drinks make you feel cool?
2. Members of your group are "drink designers." Each member should think of a new and different drink that shows his or her personality. Give each drink a name, list its ingredients, and describe its effects.
3. Pretend you are anthropology students comparing drinking beliefs and customs around the world. Choose a culture and describe a popular drink and customs associated with that drink.

Optional: Write your answers to the Recycle activities.

Threads

The warmth of the sun can be used to brew tea. Set tea and cold water in a glass container in the sun for four hours. Serve over ice.

Review

The following pairs of words have either similar or different meanings. Circle **S** or **D** in the left column.

S	D	**1.** drink	beverage
S	D	**2.** rare	common
S	D	**3.** informal	casual
S	D	**4.** always	seldom
S	D	**5.** smell	aroma
S	D	**6.** casual	formal
S	D	**7.** host	guest
S	D	**8.** sometimes	occasionally
S	D	**9.** nervous	relaxed
S	D	**10.** habit	custom

Test Yourself

Test your knowledge of the meanings of words from this chapter by taking the following quiz. Circle the letter before the word that correctly completes the following sentences.

1. Ashraf's _____ time of day is in the afternoon, after classes, when he can relax at a coffee shop and meet his friends.

   a. casual   **b.** favorite

2. Meeting at the coffee shop is a _____ way for students to get together.

   a. common   **b.** rare

3. This coffee shop is open all day. The _____ from this coffee shop are strong and inviting.

   a. guests   **b.** smells

4. The coffee shop _____ strong, fresh coffee.

   a. smells   **b.** serves

5. Ashraf likes the coffee shop because after he pays for his first cup, _____ are free.

   a. guests   **b.** refills

6. The _____ of drinking coffee is not new to Ashraf; he drinks coffee daily when he is at home in his native country.

   a. custom   **b.** host

7. In Egypt, Ashraf _____ his own coffee in a small Turkish coffeemaker.

   a. brews   **b.** hosts

8. If he has _____, he serves them coffee.

   a. smells   **b.** guests

9. Turkish coffee has a strong, almost bitter _____.

   a. flavor   **b.** habit

10. Ashraf is living in a different country while he is studying, but his _____ is the same.

    a. habit   **b.** host

Look Back

What are the most important things you learned about drinks in this chapter?

_____

_____

_____

_____

_____

Look Ahead

What else do you want to learn about drinks? How will you do this? What strategies will you use?

_____

_____

_____

_____

_____

Fun: What Do You Like To Do?

7

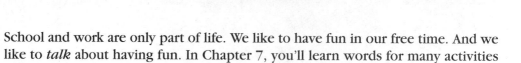

FREE TIME ACTIVITIES

School and work are only part of life. We like to have fun in our free time. And we like to *talk* about having fun. In Chapter 7, you'll learn words for many activities and sports.

PART 1: WORDS IN CONTEXT

Take a Look

What do *you* like to do? In small groups, brainstorm for types of activities people do for fun or self-improvement. Organize the activities into the following categories:

Team Sports

_____

_____

_____

_____

Music

_____

_____

_____

_____

Art

_____

_____

_____

_____

Health and Fitness

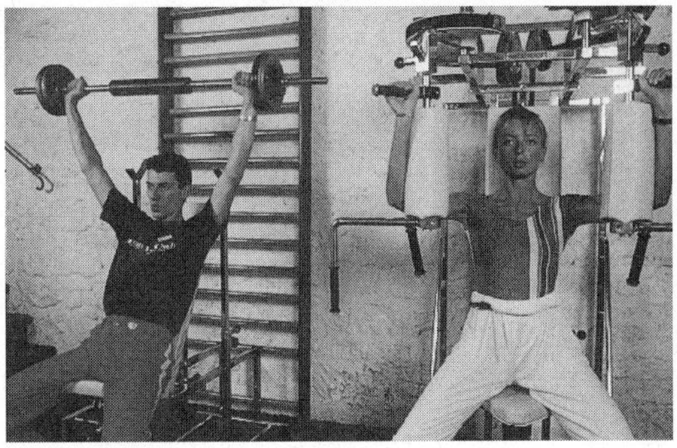

Dance

Lifestyle

Threads

Dr. James Naismith invented basketball in 1892.

The Ethnic Almanac

Career

Education

IT WORKS! Learning Strategy: Brainstorming for New Words

Other

Read About It

Following is an excerpt from a community center activity schedule. Read it and then answer the questions that follow.

MONROEVILLE COMMUNITY CENTER
934 Center Street

- Volleyball for Adults
  Co-Ed
  Beg–Adv, Tues. 6:00–7:30 PM

- Basketball
  Co-Ed Pick-Up Games
  Thurs, 6:00–7:30 PM

- Jazz Dance
  Mon & Wed 7:30–9:00 AM

- Beginning /Intermediate Ballet
  Mon & Wed 7:30–9:00 AM

- Advanced Ballet
  Tues & Thurs 7:30–9:00 AM

- Tai Kwan Do
  Intermediate/Advanced
  Tues & Thurs 6:00–8:30 PM

- Aerobics for Everybody
  Thurs 10:00–10:30 AM

- Yoga
  Beginners welcome.
  Tues 6:15–7:30 PM

- Stress Management
  Thurs 7:30–9:00 PM

- Weight Management
  Thurs 7:30–9:30 PM

- Creative Ceramics
  Weds 7:00–9:30 PM

- Adult Swim Lessons
  Mon–Fri 8:00–8:30 PM.

- Job Search Workshop:
  How To Write a Resumé
  3/16–4/20
  Weds 6:30–8:30 PM

Check Your Understanding

Answer these questions about the information in the community center schedule:

1. When can you play basketball?

   _____

   _____

2. You want to take ballet, and you've never taken it before. On which day will you take it?

   _____

   _____

3. If you want to learn how to relax, which class will you take?

_____

_____

IT WORKS!
Learning Strategy:
Putting information
into Categories

4. If you want to lose weight, which class will you take?

_____

_____

5. If you want to look for a job, which class will you take?

_____

_____

6. Put the activities in this schedule into categories:

Team Sports

_____

_____

_____

_____

Exercise Classes

_____

_____

_____

_____

Art Classes

_____

_____

_____

_____

Dance

_____

_____

_____

_____

Martial Arts

_____

_____

_____

_____

Health and Stress Management

_____

_____

_____

_____

Career Management

_____

_____

_____

_____

Other

_____

_____

_____

_____

Word Bank

Here are the new words for this chapter. They are organized into three groups: Activities, Types of Classes, and Verbs. Add them to your Word Journal.

LEARNING STRATEGY

Forming Concepts: Learning new words in related groups helps you better understand their meanings.

Threads

Aerobics is a system of physical conditioning designed to improve respiratory and circulatory function.

Webster's Ninth New College Dictionary

ACTIVITIES

volleyball	basketball	yoga	aerobics
tae kwan do	ceramics	ballet	jazz dance
weight lifting	martial arts	team sports	fitness
swimming	soccer	baseball	piano
guitar	singing	resumé writing	
stress management	weight management	career management	

Questions
❶ The words listed are all nouns—names of activities. Which have an *-ing* ending?
❷ Which words look like they might not come from English?

Answers

❶ *Weight lifting, swimming, singing,* and *resumé writing* end in *-ing* because they come from verbs (*to lift weights, to swim, to sing,* and *to write*).

❷ *Tae kwan do*—Chinese; *yoga*—Hindi; *ballet*—French; *piano*—Italian.

TYPES OF CLASSES

workshop	co-ed	beginning	intermediate	advanced

Question
❸ What do you think *co-ed* means?

Answer

❸ *Co-ed* is short for *co-educational,* originally meaning "educating males and females together." Nowadays, it refers to any activity males and females do together.

VERBS

take (a class) do (yoga) practice (tae kwan do)
play (a sport) learn (piano)

Question

❹ Which activity nouns follow *take*? Which follow *play*? Which follow *do*?
Which follow *learn*? *Practice*?

Answer

❹ *take* + all, as in "a class"
play + games, team sports, and instruments, as in:
volleyball, baseball, basketball, piano, soccer, guitar, team sports
do + all, except instruments (piano, guitar) and stress or weight
management
learn + all
practice + all

PART 2: WORD EXTENSIONS

Word Forms

What do you call someone who plays baseball? What do you call someone who
plays the piano? In the following chart, write the name for the person who does
the activity in the column on the left. Use these words.

swimmer guitarist volleyball player singer ceramicist
dancer weight lifter ballerina martial artist basketball player

ACTIVITY	PERSON WHO DOES IT
volleyball	_____
martial arts	_____
swimming	_____
guitar	_____
ceramics	_____
basketball	_____
singing	_____
ballet	_____
dance	_____
weight lifting	_____

72

Pronunciation of -s Endings

When you add -s to a noun, you make it plural. But you can pronounce the -s three different ways. The pronunciation depends on the word's final sound before you added the -s.

Take a look at these examples:

Singular	Plural	Sound
sport	sports	[s]
co-ed	co-eds	[z]
base	bases	[əz]

Can you guess why the -s ending sound changes for these three words?

Generalizations:

- When a noun ends in a voiceless consonant, the -s ending sounds like [s].

    Voiceless consonants: p, t, k, th

- When a noun ends in a voiced consonant or a vowel, the -s ending sounds like [z].

    Voiced consonants: d, b, g, th
    Vowels: a, e, i, o, u

- When a noun ends in -s -z, -ch, -sh, -j, the -s ending sounds like [əz].

Practice these sounds. Tell your partner what you like to do, and what you don't like to do. Use the following plural nouns:

do aerobics	take dance classes	play team sports
do ceramics	take (or practice) martial arts	write resumés

Use Words Creatively

1. Work with a partner. Write the names of additional activities and classes you can do or take for fun and improvement:

Career Management

_____

_____

_____

_____

Health

_____

_____

_____

_____

Fitness

_____

_____

_____

_____

Personal Development

_____

_____

_____

_____

Sports

_____

_____

_____

_____

Other

_____

_____

_____

_____

2. What equipment or materials do you need to do some of the activities mentioned in this chapter? Work with a partner. Sort through the basket of jumbled up equipment and materials. Then match them with the following activities. (You might be able to use some things for more than one activity.)

basket gloves helmet
mitt potter's wheel
basketball soccer ball
barre
shin guards bat bathing suit
diving board
weights clock goal
mirror
tights swimming pool
baseball clay music

For baseball, you use:

_____ _____ _____

For basketball, you use:

_____ _____ _____

For ballet, you use:

_____ _____ _____

For piano playing, you use:

_____ _____ _____

For weight lifting, you use:

_____ _____ _____

For ceramics, you use:

_____ _____ _____

For soccer, you use:

_____ _____ _____

For aerobics, you use:

_____ _____ _____

For singing, you use:

_____ _____ _____

For swimming, you use:

_____ _____ _____

What activities don't require special equipment or materials?

_____

_____

_____

_____

_____

_____

3. In small groups, choose and discuss one or more of the following topics:
    • Why do people take exercise classes?
    • Why do people take career management classes?
    • Can an adult learn to speak a foreign language fluently? If so, what's the best way?
    • Can an adult learn to play the piano or other instrument well? If so, what's the best way?
    • Can an adult learn to dance ballet? How well? What's the best way for an adult to learn to dance?
    • Why do people study martial arts?

    One person in the group will be the note-taker and one will be the reporter. When you are finished, have the reporter tell your group's answers to the class.
4. Write a paragraph about one of the following:
    • Your favorite leisure time activity, and why you like it.
    • An area of your life you want to improve, and how you will improve it.
    • A class you took that changed your life.

Word Game

CHARADES

Play Charades. Write all the activity words from the Word Bank (and others you learned in this chapter) on index cards. Put the cards face down on a desk. Then form teams. A member of one team picks a card from the pile. He or she must act out the activity for the other team. Once someone guesses the activity, it is the other team's turn to pick a card.

Recycle

Do at least one of the following activities in small groups. Combine words from this chapter with words from previous chapters.

1. Plan a class picnic. Discuss the food, drinks, and activities you will have.
2. You are going to start a recreation center in a big city. Think of different types of activities for the entire year, in all kinds of weather: for example, think of what you can do when it rains, when it snows, when it's warm, etc.
3. You are a world traveler. You are talking to a group of students. Describe the most popular sports and activities in eight of the countries you have visited.
4. You are a job counselor. Tell a group of job seekers what jobs you can do that involve sports, and what types of people do best at these jobs.

Optional: Write your answers to the Recycle activities.

Review

Work with a partner. Review the meanings of the words on the cards you made for Charades in Part 3. (Make extra sets of cards, if necessary.) Put the cards face down on a desk. Take turns choosing a card. Make up a sentence for the word you choose. Make sure the sentence shows you know the meaning of the word.

EXAMPLE baseball —————>"We can't play baseball today because we don't have a bat and a ball."

Test Yourself

Test your knowledge of the meanings of the words in this chapter by taking the following quiz. Circle the letter before the word or phrase that best completes the sentence.

LEARNING STRATEGY

Overcoming Limitations: Practicing with multiple choice tests helps you do better on these tests.

1. If you want to learn how to relax, take
   a. resumé writing.
   b. stress management.
   c. team sports.
2. If you want to exercise with men and women, take a(n) _____ class.
   a. advanced
   b. co-ed
   c. beginning
3. If you want to lose weight, take a _____ workshop.
   a. career management
   b. ceramics
   c. weight management
4. If you like team sports, try
   a. piano.
   b. aerobics.
   c. basketball.
5. In my free time, I like to do
   a. piano.
   b. guitar.
   c. tae kwan do.

6. A person who plays the piano is a
   a. piano.
   b. pianist.
   c. pianer.
7. A person who plays volleyball is a
   a. volleyballer.
   b. ballvolleyer.
   c. volleyball player.
8. If you play soccer, you need a ball and a
   a. goal.
   b. diving board.
   c. a mirror.
9. If you do ballet, you need
   a. weights.
   b. music.
   c. a basket.
10. Tae kwan do is a
    a. soft drink.
    b. martial art.
    c. team sport.

Look Back

What did you learn about activities for fun and self-improvement?

_____

_____

_____

_____

_____

Look Ahead

What else do you want to learn about activities for fun and self-improvement? How do you plan to do this?

_____

_____

_____

_____

_____

Games: What Do You Like to Play?

Think about the games you played as a child. Did you play card games, sports, or board games? You play board games on a playing surface or game board. In this chapter, you will learn some words and expressions for describing international board games.

 PART 1: WORDS IN CONTEXT

Threads

The first recorded game is Senet, a popular game in ancient Egypt 4,000 years ago. It is probably the ancestor of Backgammon.

Take a Look

The following drawings show game boards for games from around the world. With a partner, try to guess the names of the games. (You may think of more than one game for a game board.) Write the names of the games on the lines.

1. _____

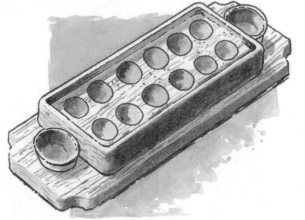

2. _____

3. _____

4. _____

Forming Concepts: Linking diagrams with words helps you learn and remember new words.

Read About It

Mankala is an ancient game for children and adults from many parts of Africa and the Middle East. It is one of the most popular board games in the world. The rules are simple but players must use strategy to win. How do you play Mankala? Read these directions for one version of this game.

MANKALA: A Game of Strategy

Use a Mankala game board. Two players need 40 playing pieces. These are called Hasa in some areas. You can use buttons, beads, or marbles. They should all be about the same size and shape.

- Player 1 begins in the top left hole by putting more than two but less than five Hasa in each of the 12 holes until all 40 Hasa are used. The player does not have to put the same number of Hasa in each hole.
- When Player 1 is finished, Player 2 starts in the bottom right hole by picking up all the Hasa in this hole and starting with the next hole to the right, dropping one Hasa at a time into each successive hole.
- When he drops his last piece in, he checks the number of Hasa in this last hole. If it now contains two or four Hasa, this player takes all the Hasa in the hole on the opposite side of the game board and puts them in his or her cup on the end of the board.
- Player 2 continues playing around the game board. He returns to the last hole where he dropped the last Hasa. He picks up all the Hasa in this hole and continues around the board until he drops his last Hasa. Then he checks again to see how many Hasa are in this last hole. If there are two or four, again he wins the Hasa in the opposite hole.
- He continues playing until he drops his last Hasa into an empty hole. Then it is Player 1's turn. This player begins from his starting hole and continues around the board in the same way. If the starting hole is empty the players should begin at the next hole to the right. He will put the Hasa he wins into his or her cup at the end of the board.
- The game is finished when too few Hasa remain on the board for a player to win. The player with the most Hasa in his cup at the end of the game wins.

Threads

Mankala rewards the thoughtful planner every time.

The Board Book of Class Games

Check Your Understanding

1. Circle **T** if the sentence is true and **F** if it is false.

   T   F   **a.** The directions are for three players.

   T   F   **b.** You need 40 playing pieces for Mankala.

   T   F   **c.** You can use buttons, beads, or marbles for playing pieces.

   T   F   **d.** Each player begins in a different hole.

   T   F   **e.** There are 10 holes on the Mankala game board.

   T   F   **f.** You play the game by dropping playing pieces into successive holes.

   T   F   **g.** Both players move playing pieces at the same time.

   T   F   **h.** If your last hole contains two or four playing pieces, you can take them.

   T   F   **i.** If your last hole contains two or four playing pieces, you can take the pieces in the hole on the opposite side of the game board.

   T   F   **j.** The player with the least playing pieces at the end of the game wins.

2. Use these labels to complete the diagram.

   Mankala game board   Direction of play
   Player 1 starting hole   Player 1 cup
   Player 2 starting hole   Player 2 cup

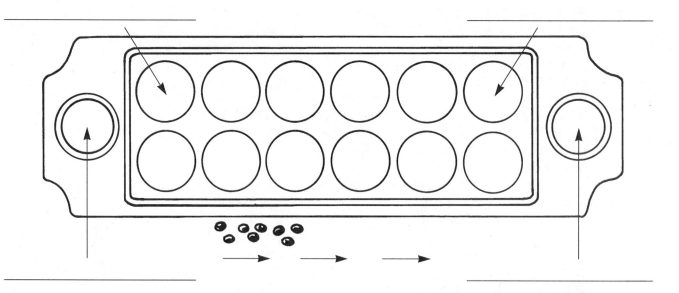

Word Bank

Here are the words presented in this chapter. Add them to your Word Journal.

PLAYING GAMES

1	2	3	4
gameboard	win	rules	bottom
playing pieces	drop	team	challenging
marbles	begin	direction	first
buttons	lose	skill	last
beads	block	instructions	full
cup	take turns	strategy	successive
top	remain	opponent	opposite
hole	contain	luck	
square	plan		
team member			

LEARNING STRATEGY

**Forming Concepts: Guessing promotes your language
comprehension.**

Questions

1. What is similar between the pronunciation of *successive* and *instruction?*
2. Opposite and opponent both have three syllables. Is the *oppo* in both words pronounced the same?
3. *Whole* is a homonym (word with same pronunciation, different meaning) for which word in the Word Bank?
4. What are the verb forms of these three nouns: *direction, instructions, challenging?*
5. The words in this Word Bank are arranged in four columns: 1, 2, 3, and 4. With a partner, decide what the words in each column have in common. Then give each column a title.

Answers

1. The first *c* in *successive* and the *c* in *instruction* are pronounced [k]. In addition, the second syllable is stressed in both words.
2. No. The first syllable of opposite is stressed while the second syllable of opponent is stressed.
3. *hole*
4. *direct, instruct, challenge*
5. Here are some suggestions for column titles:
   Column 1: Nouns—Objects You Need for Games
   Column 2: Verbs—What Players Do When They Play Games
   Column 3: Nouns—These Make Games Fair and Fun
   Column 4: Adjectives—Words That Describe Games: order, parts, positions, etc.

Spelling Numbers

It is important to be able to recognize and write the correct spelling of numbers. Numbers from 1–100 are written below. Rewrite them in order in the chart. Begin with one.

twelve	eighteen	thirteen		
one	ten	eleven	two	
twenty	three	thirty		
four	fourteen	forty	one hundred	
five	fifty	seventeen	six	
sixty	seven	seventy	eight	
eighty	nine	ninety	fifteen	

1	2	3	4	5
6	7	8	9	10
11	12	13	14	15
16	17	18	19	20
30	40	50	60	70
80	90	100		

1. Without looking at your chart, write homonyms (words with the same pronunciation but different spelling) for *won, to, fore,* and *ate.*

2. Which numbers do not follow regular spelling patterns?

3. Which numbers are difficult to spell?

Listing Signals

When explaining or writing a process, it is useful to use listing signals to make the
order of steps clear. Study these listing signals then answer the questions.

First,
Next,
Then,
After that,
Later,
Last,
Finally,
At the end,

1. With a partner, describe your early development
   as a child. When did you learn to talk, walk, and
   eat by yourself? Use listing signals.
2. Explain to your partner how to play a simple
   children's game.
3. What are the first three important things to do when learning a foreign
   language?

Directions

It is useful to learn words that describe **ways to move** playing pieces on a
gameboard. Study the list of words and the arrows, then do the activity.

DIRECTIONS

around ↻

to the right →

to the left ←

up ↑

down ↓

forward (usually from start toward finish)

backward (usually from finish toward start)

horizontally ↔

vertically ↕

diagonally ↗ ↘

Choose a gameboard for a
game at the beginning of the
chapter. With your partner, take
turns giving directions for that
game. Use your finger or the
tip of your pen or pencil as a
playing piece.

Use Words Creatively

1. Teach someone in your class how to play one of your favorite games. Choose one of the games from Part 1 or another game you know. Bring the gameboard and playing pieces to class. Use new words from this chapter.
2. Write the rules to a game you know and like. Follow the example of the steps presented for Mankala. Have a student read your directions and tell you if they are clear and easy to understand.

_____: A game of _____

Use a _____ gameboard. _____ players

need _____ playing pieces. These are called _____.

You can use _____. They should all be _____.

- Player 1 begins _____ by _____.
- When Player 1 is finished, Player 2 starts _____ by
  _____.
- When he _____, he _____.
  If _____, then _____.
- _____
  _____
- _____
  _____
- The game is finished when _____. The player
  _____ at the end of the game wins.

Threads

Chinese checkers, which became popular in the United States in the 1930s, did not come from China.

3. Ask three people outside of class about their favorite games. Present your results to the class.

Word Game

JEOPARDY

This is a version of a popular game on television. Divide into two teams. Take turns providing answers. Each correct question wins a point. There is more than one question for each answer. The team with the most points at the end of the game wins.

EXAMPLE   Answer: marbles
Question: What are playing pieces in Chinese Checkers?

Answers

1. a gameboard
2. careful planning
3. Player 1 loses the game
4. how to play the game
5. it's easy
6. many players working together
7. round or square
8. to begin the game
9. luck and skill
10. move playing pieces across the board

Recycle

Do at least one of the following activities in small groups. Combine words from this chapter with words from previous chapters.

1. Design a simple board game relating to your school or community. Draw a map and numbered boxes on a playing board so that a player can work his or her way from place to place by rolling a die and moving a playing piece. Write the directions to your game.
2. Pretend you are a market analyst (someone who studies possible customers for a new product). Choose one popular game and describe the personality and habits of someone who would really like this game.

Optional: Write your answers to the Recycle activities.

Review

The words in the following lists are either **antonyms** or **synonyms.** Draw a - - - - - line between the pairs of antonyms and a + + + + line between the pairs of synonyms.

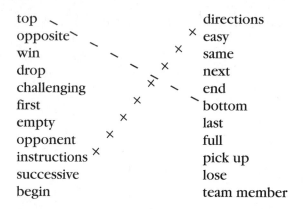

top	directions
opposite	easy
win	same
drop	next
challenging	end
first	bottom
empty	last
opponent	full
instructions	pick up
successive	lose
begin	team member

Test Yourself

Use the words in the list to complete the paragraphs about Checkers.

opposite	first
begins	playing pieces
12	diagonally
forward	gameboard
players	squares

Checkers is a game played by two _____ 1 with round _____ 2 , called checkers. Each player has _____ 3 checkers. One set is red, the other is black. The _____ 4 has 64 black and red _____ 5 arranged in a checkered pattern. The players sit on _____ 6 sides of the board and arrange their checkers on the _____ 7 three rows of black squares.

The player with the black checkers _____ 8 . Players can only move checkers one space _____ 9 or _____ 10 toward the opposite side of the board. They can only move on black squares.

LEARNING STRATEGY

Overcoming Limitations: Writing the answers that you know first will help you build confidence and save time.

Look Back

What are the most important things you learned about games in this chapter?

_____

_____

_____

_____

Look Ahead

What else do you want to learn about games? How will you do this? What strategies will you use?

_____

_____

_____

_____

Tools: Which Do You Need?

Tools are objects that help us do something. **Simple tools** help us open, close, push, pull, hold, and do many other tasks. **Complex tools** help us build, destroy, communicate, and even think. In this chapter, you will learn the names of **simple tools** and think about the tools we use everyday—at home, at work, in school.

LEARNING STRATEGY

Forming Concepts: Thinking about words you already know prepares you for learning new material.

Before you begin Chapter 9, take a moment with your classmates to think about some synonyms for the word *tool* that you have spoken, heard, or read. Write as many synonyms as you can think of in the key below:

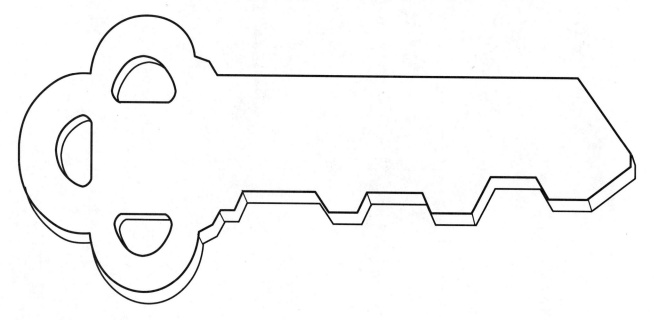

Threads

A tool is anything necessary for doing one's job.

Here are some synonyms for the word ***tool:*** *gadget, instrument, device. Apparatus* is another synonym for *tool* that is used less frequently. Add these synonyms and others you found to your key.

Take a Look

Think about the simple tools you use everyday. Think about the tools that are **not** mechanical or electrical and those that most people have in their homes. Look at the sketches of rooms and places. Make a list of the tools you use in these places.

1. Kitchen

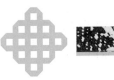

2. Bathroom

_____

_____

_____

4. Workshop

_____

_____

_____

3. Bus

_____

_____

_____

_____

_____

_____

5. Add a place, draw a sketch, and add the tools you use there:

_____

_____

_____

93

Read About It

What do you need when you move into an apartment? You will read a page from a catalog that lists some items everyone needs in their home. Look at the pictures, then read the names and descriptions for each of the items.

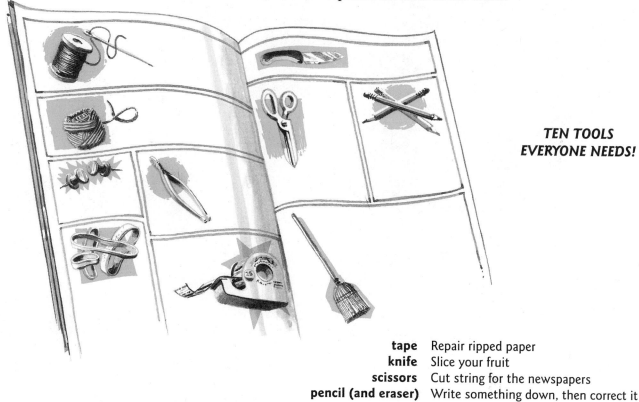

*TEN TOOLS
EVERYONE NEEDS!*

tape	Repair ripped paper
knife	Slice your fruit
scissors	Cut string for the newspapers
pencil (and eraser)	Write something down, then correct it
broom	Sweep the floor

needle (and thread)	Be ready for missing buttons
string	Tie up old newspapers
thumbtack	Put notices and posters on your wall
rubber band	Keep your things together
tweezers	Pull out splinters

Check Your Understanding

1. Answer these questions about the items described above.
    a. Are the items large or small? Which can fit into a drawer or a small bag? Which can not? Write **L** next to large items or **S** next to small items.
    b. Which tools in the list can hurt someone who is not careful? Write **D** next to the item if it can be dangerous.
    c. Which tools in the list are expensive? Which are inexpensive? Write **E** next to expensive items and **I** next to inexpensive items.
    d. Which tool in the list is the most important? Which tool could you not live without? Choose the most important tool and explain to your classmates why it is so important.
    e. Add two more important tools to the catalog page. Sketch the items, label them, and describe what they do.
    f. Do you agree that the ten tools listed are the ones that everyone needs? Pretend that a friend is moving into her own place. You and your partner want to give her ten tools she will need. Make your own list of ten tools. Present it to your class.

Personalizing: Adding your own ideas to learning material increases your motivation.

2. Another way to think about the everyday tools you use is to review the **functions** (purposes) they have. Write an everyday tool in the left column for each of the functions in the right column. Work with your classmates to complete this chart.

TOOL	FUNCTION
_____	attach
_____	close
_____	cut
_____	dry
_____	hold
_____	open
_____	pound
_____	pull
_____	reflect
_____	scoop
_____	screw
_____	sew
_____	stir
_____	tie
_____	twist
_____	write

Threads

There are claw hammers, bricklayer's hammers, stone hammers, sledge hammers, mechanic's hammers and riveting hammers.

Managing Your Learning: Looking at new words and ideas from many perspectives makes your learning thorough.

3. Now think about the tasks (jobs) you do with everyday tools. For each task on the left, write the tool on the right. If you can, add some tasks and tools that are not on the list.

TASKS When you want to . . .	TOOLS You need a . . .
1. remove a splinter	_____
2. sew on a button	_____
3. unlock a door	_____
4. tie some sticks together	_____
5. cut a piece of paper	_____
6. write a note	_____
7. stick paper to paper	_____
8. cut some bread	_____
9. dry a dish	_____
10. replace the screw in your glasses	_____
11. hold together two pieces of wood	_____
12. remove a nail	_____
13. scoop some sugar	_____
14. see yourself	_____
15. eat a piece of meat	_____
16. _____	_____
17. _____	_____
18. _____	_____
19. _____	_____
20. _____	_____

Threads

Twine, or string, is made from sisal fiber from the agave plant. This plant, sometimes referred to as the Century plant, is plentiful in parts of East Africa.

LEARNING STRATEGY

Remembering New Material: Keeping a Word Journal helps you learn new words and review old words.

Word Bank

Here are the new words presented in this chapter. Add them to your Word Journal.

EVERYDAY HAND TOOLS

_____	_____
hammer	pound, hit
screwdriver	twist, turn
wrench	pull
pin	stick, poke
(thumb) tack	pierce
needle	sew
rubber band	stretch
pencil	write
knife	cut, slice, sharpen, shave, carve
fork	stab
key	open
spoon	scoop, stir, mix
towel	rub, dry, absorb
mirror	reflect
stick	hit
string	tie
wire	bend, hold
tape	attach, stick

Questions

① Each of the columns in the Word Bank has a title. One is *Tools* and the other is *Functions*. What is the correct title for each column? Write the correct one at the top of each column.

② How many syllables do *towel* and *mirror* have?

③ Are the *u*'s in *pull* and *cut* pronounced the same?

④ What are two other words not from the Word Bank that rhyme (have the same vowel sound) as sew?

⑤ What two similarities (in meaning and pronunciation) can you find between *knife* and *needle?*

Answers

⑤ Both words begin with \n\ and both are sharp.

④ Go, no, toe, low, etc.

③ No. \pul\ and \kət\

② They each have two syllables: tow•el and mir•ror

① *Tools* is the title of the left column; *Functions* is the title of the right column.

Countable/Noncountable Pairs

Everyday hand tools are either countable, noncountable, or referred to as a pair. If a tool is countable, it is preceded by *a, an* or *the* if it is singular. It is followed by *-s* if it is plural. If it is noncountable, it is preceded by *the, some,* or nothing and never takes an *-s*. If a tool is regarded as a pair, it is preceded by *some, a pair of* or nothing. Study the chart below to review how these words are used. Then, with a partner, write five true sentences about the way you use everyday hand tools.

TYPE OF NOUN	HOW IT IS USED	EVERYDAY HAND TOOLS	
COUNTABLE	I bought **a hammer** at the hardware store.	fork hammer key knife mirror needle pen/pencil pin rubber band	screwdriver spoon stick string tape thumbtack wire wrench
NONCOUNTABLE	She tied **some string** around the sticks.	string wire	tape
CONSIDERED A PAIR	I used **a pair of tweezers** to remove the thorn.	pliers tweezers	scissors

Associated Meanings

Look at these groups of words with similar meanings. One word in each group does not have an associated, or similar, meaning or application. Circle this word, then talk about how the other words in the group are related. There may be more than one associated meaning or application for each group of words. Think about what the tools do, how they work, and who uses them.

> **EXAMPLE** needle   hammer   pin   knife
> *Hammer* does not fit in this group.
> The other words refer to tools that are sharp.

1. wrench	screwdriver	key	spoon	
2. hit	pound	push	rub	
3. stretch	hold	pull	tie	
4. splinter	button	lock	nail	towel
5. kitchen	gadget	instrument	tool	
6. eraser	towel	mirror		
7. fork	knife	spoon	rubber band	
8. cut	open	slice	stab	
9. baby	student	carpenter	cook	
10. towel	knife	fork	spoon	hammer

Use Words Creatively

1. Describe the tools you use everyday. Write a paragraph describing what you do, then read it to your classmates. Try to include at least ten tools in your description. Use the categories below to help you develop your paragraph.

TIME	PLACE	FUNCTION	TOOL

LEARNING STRATEGY

Overcoming Limitations: Singing new words enhances your memory.

2. Peter, Paul, and Mary have been singing *If I Had a Hammer* for many years. Help them develop some new lyrics for their song. Add three tools and tasks to the familiar tune by following their pattern, then sing your updated version of the song with your class.

If I had a hammer, I'd hammer in the morning. . . .

If I had a _____, I'd _____ when/where/how

Word Games

TALKATIVE TOOLS

Choose two of the everyday tools you've thought about in this chapter and give them human qualities. Write a conversation between your tools and share it with your classmates.

LEARNING STRATEGY

Understanding and Using Emotions: Including emotions in conversations with other students helps you understand each other and builds trust.

THREE TOOLS TO SAVE

Uh-oh! There is a fire in the place where you live. You have enough time to gather your valuables and **three** hand tools you think you will need. Which three hand tools do you choose and why?

PANTOMIME

Pretend you are a tool. Act out what you are and what you do in front of the class without speaking. Try to help them guess which tool you are.

Threads

Early humans used stone tools to pierce, scrape, cut, smash, and dig.

Recycle

Do at least one of the following activities in small groups. Combine words from this chapter with words from previous chapters.

1. Certain kinds of foods or food preparations require special tools. Pretend that you are a kitchen store owner and that you are trying to stock your store with kitchen supplies for ethnic cooking. Suggest a special tool (and the food with which it is used) to sell in your store.

2. You are planning an automobile trip around the United States with a group of classmates. Recommend five emergency tools for this trip.

3. Pretend you are a travel agent. One of your clients is travelling to Hawaii (where the weather is generally warm) and another client is travelling to the Antarctic (where it is always cold). Recommend five travel tools that will help each client be safe and comfortable.

Optional: Write your answers to the Recycle activities.

PART 4: ASSESSMENT

TOOLS	FUNCTIONS
1. hammer	pull
2. tape	stir
3. needle	write
4. tweezers	dry
5. screwdriver	cut
6. scissors	open
7. pencil	screw
8. spoon	pound
9. towel	attach
10. key	sew

Review

Match the tool to its function in as little time as possible.

Test Yourself

Recall the names and functions of everyday hand tools by solving the following problems. Read the problem, describe the task you will do, and identify the tool.

PROBLEM	YOU NEED TO . . .	YOU WILL USE . . .
1. You're all wet.		
2. Your toenails are too long.		
3. The piece of bread is too big to eat.		
4. You have a thorn in your finger.		
5. You need to take a phone message.		
6. Your shirt is torn.		
7. Your suitcase is locked and you want to open it.		
8. The cassette player is missing a screw.		
9. Your photo came off your ID card.		
10. The newspapers you want to recycle need to be organized.		

Look Back

What did you learn about everyday hand tools and their functions in this chapter?

_____

_____

_____

_____

_____

Look Ahead

What else do you want to learn about everyday hand tools? How do you plan to do it?

_____

_____

_____

_____

_____

Tools: Can Computers Help You Learn?

COMPUTERS: TOOLS FOR THE 1990s

What are important tools for students? Long ago, only books, paper, pencils, and pens were important student tools. But nowadays there are many electronic aids to help students learn fast and easily. In this chapter, you will learn some words and expressions for talking about computers.

PART 1: WORDS IN CONTEXT

Take a Look

What do you think is the most important tool for a student? Some people believe it is the personal computer. Do you agree? Discuss the answer to this question with your classmates. Then look at the following photo. With a classmate label as many parts of the photo as you can.

Threads

The machine that can make hard things easy is the educator.

Adapted from Ralph Waldo Emerson

_____

_____

_____

_____

_____

104

Read About It

The following flyer is from a computer store.
Read it, then answer the questions.

BE SUCCESSFUL IN SCHOOL, AT WORK, AT HOME!

BUY A COMPUTER!

BLOWOUT SALE THIS WEEK!

Add memory to the computer system you already have

Many economical software bundles

Make charts, tables, business reports and spreadsheets

The best integrated software for word processing and accounting

Ask about discounts on laptops and notebooks

Monitors with vivid color display

Choose from new fonts to make your text documents attractive and easy to read

Tutorials with all software programs

Standard and extended keyboards for your desktop computers

Use a mouse or function keys

Lots of graphic applications

Check Your Understanding

1. Complete these sentences with words from the flyer.
   a. A TV for a computer is called a

   _____.

   b. Charts, tables, and graphs are called

   _____.

   c. A _____ is the letter style you choose to use.

   d. If a computer has a lot of _____, you can save many documents on its hard drive.

   e. You can control what you do on a computer by clicking and dragging with a _____.

Managing Your Learning: Organizing new words in charts helps you use them correctly.

2. Following are some more words from the flyer. Mark whether each word refers to **hardware** (computer *machinery*) or **software** (*systems* that control a computer).

THIS WORD	REFERS TO	HARDWARE	SOFTWARE
monitor		X	_____
spreadsheets		_____	_____
mouse		_____	_____
word processing		_____	_____
memory		_____	_____
fonts		_____	_____
application		_____	_____
graphics		_____	_____
keyboard		_____	_____

Word Bank

Here are the new words presented in this chapter. Add them to your Word Journal.

COMPUTERS AND LEARNING

bundle	icon
document	keyboard
file	monitor
application	notebook
button	laptop
charts	memory
command	menu
component	merge
desktop	modem
display	mouse
e-mail	multimedia
export	personal computer
font	program
function	software
graphics	spreadsheets
import	text
integrated software	tutorial
interactive videodisk	word processing

Threads

Think and Talk French, as a multimedia learning program, allows you to learn French by playing with the language. It helps you to think in French.

Reviewed by Jeff Eaton,
Spring 1994

Questions

1. *Compound words* are words made up of two smaller words. Keyboard is made from *key* and *board* and is a compound word. How many other compound words can you find in the Word Bank?

2. Many computer words are international, that is, the English version is used in all languages. How many words from the Word Bank do not have an equivalent (translation) in your native language?

3. What do you think the *e* represents in *e-mail?*

4. What do these words have in common: *command, display, export, file, function, import,* and *program?*

5. Which words from the Word Bank have you seen before in a different setting? For example, menu refers to a list of choices on your computer as well as in a restaurant. Make a list of words you have seen in a different context.

Answers

5. Answers will vary.

4. They can be used as both nouns and verbs.

3. *electronic*

2. Answers depend on students' native languages.

1. *notebook, desktop, laptop, mainframe, multimedia, spreadsheet, joystick.*

Versatile Words

In Part 1 you listed words that you have seen before in a context not related to computers. These words are **versatile** because you can use them in two or more contexts. Look at the words below and think about how they are used in two contexts. Then make up six of your own sentences using these words in different ways. Share your sentences with your classmates when you are finished.

VERSATILE WORDS	WITH COMPUTERS	OTHER CONTEXT(S)
application	software program **EXAMPLE** *Mariella needs an application that will integrate graphics and word processing.*	form required for employment, college **EXAMPLE** *Peter turned in his application to the university last month.*
bundle	software programs sold together	group of clothes, laundry
import/export	move words or pictures from one file, program, document to another	bring business products in to a state or country or send out from a state or country
integrated	different systems that can work together	people from different ethnic origins that live/work/study together
menu	a list of choices within a program	the list of food options in a restaurant
merge	combine data from one or more files	join a traffic lane on a freeway or highway
notebook	portable computer	binder, collection of paper, primarily used by students
tutorial	a computer program that teaches how to do something	one-on-one teaching

Computer Verbs

Computers and high tech tools have generated a specialized list of words that have particular meanings in this new context. There are many functions a computer can perform. It is useful to know the names of these functions. Study the list of verbs that describe computer functions. Put a check (✔) next to the functions **you've** performed on a computer. Add four more functions that are not listed. With a partner, explain what each function does. Finally, assign five functions a partner must do the next time she or he works on a computer.

FUNCTIONS (*COMPUTER* VERBS)

_____ click	_____ get info	_____ open	_____ save	_____
_____ close	_____ go online	_____ preview	_____ select	_____
_____ e-mail	_____ highlight	_____ print	_____ undo	
_____ find	_____ insert	_____ pull down		
_____ format	_____ merge	_____ replace		

Use Words Creatively

1. Have you ever created anything on a computer? Write about a project (report, database, art, music, a program, letter, etc.). If you haven't used a computer before, what project would you like to do on a computer? Use as many new words as possible. Share your writing with your class when you are finished.

LEARNING STRATEGY

Forming Concepts: Bringing materials to class that relate to learning increases your understanding of new vocabulary.

2. A section of your local newspaper helps people answer questions they have about computers. Readers send letters describing their questions and problems to Carla, the Computer Expert. Carla is sick this week and she has asked you and your classmates to fill in for her. Write answers to these letters. Bring in some computer magazines and catalogs to help you with this task.

a. Dear Carla,

I need a personal computer but I just can't decide which to buy. We use an IBM at work, but my children use a Macintosh in school. IBM computers are a little less expensive, but Macs are a little easier to use. Do you have advice for me?

Confused

b. Dear Carla,

My boss has just bought me a computer at work. She wants ME to choose the software. I need a good word processing program and some database software. What do you recommend?

Ready to Buy

c. Dear Carla,

I have just started taking classes at the local community college. Everyone tells me I should learn to use a computer to help me with my schoolwork but I don't know anything about them. I have never used a computer before. What's the best way to learn about computers?

Fearful Student

d. Now write a letter to Carla with a computer question of your own. Give it to another student for an answer.

LEARNING STRATEGY

Understanding and Using Emotions: Responding to a person's feelings builds a relationship of trust and increases capacity for learning.

Word Game

PASSWORD

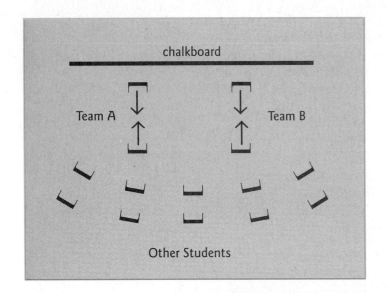

chalkboard

Team A

Team B

Other Students

Work in two teams. Put four chairs at the front of the room, two facing away from the chalkboard (towards the class) and two facing the chalkboard. Team members should face each other. The teacher or a student selects a word from the Word Bank and writes it on the board. Students facing the board read the word silently and alternate giving one-word clues to their teammates. The first person to guess the word wins points for his or her team. Students get 10 chances to guess the word. Points decrease with each turn. Students change places each time a new word is written on the board. The team with the most points at the end wins.

Recycle

Do at least one of the following activities in small groups. Combine words from this chapter with words from previous chapters.

1. In an informal conversation with your classmates, talk about your favorite computer games. Which are the most fun, most challenging, most addictive (difficult to stop)?

2. In what ways can the computer help you learn about international weather? How can the computer be helpful if you are in the food industry? Pretend you are a computer consultant. In a review of chapters from the entire book, think of at least two ways computers can be applied to each of the topics you've discussed previously. The topics are listed here.

    Geographical Areas of the World
    International Weather
    People and Professions
    Personality and Personal Style
    Food Recommendations
    International Drinking Customs
    Free Time Activities
    International Board Games
    Everyday Hand Tools

3. Pretend you can see into the future. Predict five new computer jobs (in any field) that will become available.

    Optional: Write your answers to the Recycle activities.

LEARNING STRATEGY

Overcoming Limitations: Working with a partner can be faster and more fun when doing work that is difficult.

Review

Here's a crossword puzzle reviewing the meanings and uses of words from this chapter. You will notice that a few of the clues are incomplete. First, with a partner, complete the clues. Then do the crossword puzzle. Good luck!

CROSSWORD CLUES

ACROSS

2. Documents from a computer are _____ to read.
3. Computer users organize their documents in a _____ .
4. A computer is a learning _____ .
6. The development of the _____ has changed the way students learn.
8. Many students now have a _____ computer to help them with their work.
10. A _____ enables you to communicate over phone lines.
11. If you have to do a research _____ , it is a good idea to do it on a computer.
12. Computer users store their data on a _____ .
14. _____ is communication over phone lines.
17. The computer _____ displays the computer user's work.
19. *Application* is another word for _____ .

Computer Crossword

DOWN

1. A mouse works best on a _____ .
2. Nowadays there are many _____ aids to help students learn things fast and easily.
3. A _____ is a letter style.
5. For some programs, you _____ the application by clicking on an icon.
7. Some applications refer to writing as _____ .
9. Some _____ computers can fit into a briefcase.
10. The _____ command enables a computer user to combine two documents.
13. The letter keys are located on the _____ .
15. A popular personal computer brand name is _____ .
16. _____ are symbols that represent applications, functions, or documents.
17. Computer users can choose what they want to do from a _____ .
18. Another popular brand of personal computers.

111

Test Yourself

Complete the sentences in this selection on Multimedia Computing by using the words listed before the reading. This was written to encourage people to use computers for learning.

documents   mouse   text   software   keys   programs
personal computer   multimedia   graphics   CD-ROMS

The Power of Learning with Multimedia Personal Computing

Imagine hearing Swahili being spoken, watching the dance of a honeybee, or learning about the development of the telephone by looking at pictures . . . just by clicking a _____ or hitting a few
₁
_____ on your _____ . People learn
₂   ₃
in a variety of ways, by seeing, hearing and doing. Personal computers enhance learning for parents and children. And when computer _____ offer information through pictures, written
₄
articles, sound, animation, and video—known as _____—it
₅
presents information in all the ways people really think and learn.

Multimedia computers use special compact discs like the ones you play on your stereo. But these _____—which stands for Compact
₆
Disc-Read Only Memory—offer much more than sound. They combine animation, video, photographic-quality pictures, _____
₇
and _____ in a beautiful presentation.
₈
CD ROMs store lots of information and cannot be erased or changed. But you can use information and pictures from multimedia _____
₉
in _____ you create.
₁₀
Multimedia computing can improve your "learning power" so that children and adults can have fun while exploring the world.

Adapted from The Power of Learning with
Multimedia Personal Computing from Microsoft

Look Back

What are the most important things you learned about computers in this chapter?

_____

_____

_____

_____

_____

Look Ahead

What else do you want to learn about computers? How will you do this?

_____

_____

_____

_____

_____

Answers to Selected Exercises

CHAPTER 1 PLACES: WHERE ARE YOU FROM?

Check Your Understanding   p. 3

1. If necessary, refer to an atlas or world map.
2. **a.** Latin America and the Caribbean
   b. Africa
   c. 29 percent
   d. Answers will vary.

Review   p. 9

1. Answers will vary.

Test Yourself   p. 9

1. Lebanese
2. El Salvadorean
3. French, English
4. Answers will vary. Sample answers: China, Korea
5. Eastern Europe
6. Greek
7. Italian
8. the Middle East
9. Answers will vary. Sample answers: Japan, Japanese
10. Answers will vary. Sample answers: the Middle East, Saudi Arabia, Kuwait

CHAPTER 2 PLACES: HOW'S THE WEATHER?

Check Your Understanding   p. 14

1. the Southeast, the mid-Atlantic states, the Great Lakes, the West, the Southwest
2. rain, thunderstorms, tropical storm, storm system, scattered showers, sunny, warm, dry weather conditions, thundershowers
3. • the Southeast
   • Mid-Atlantic or the Southeast or the West
   • the Great Lakes or the Mid-Atlantic or the Southeast
4. No region has snow.
5. No region has ice.

Word Game — p. 18

Weather Crossword Puzzle

```
 ¹H  I         ²S  N  O  ³W     ⁴F  O  ⁵G
 ⁶T  O     ⁷S     E        E    O     O
 ⁸T  E  M  P  E  R  ⁹R  A  T  U  R  E
¹⁰C     O        A        E
¹¹O  N  G        I        ¹²I  C  y
 O ¹³H ¹⁴W ¹⁵I  N  D  Y       A
 L  E     C              ¹⁶S  U ¹⁷N
   ¹⁸F  A  H  R  E  N ¹⁹H  E ²⁰I  T     O
       V           A     L        R
²¹D  R  Y    ²²D ²³R  I  Z  Z  L  E     T
              ²⁴N  E                 H
```

Review — p. 19

Answers will vary.

Test Yourself — p. 20

1. regions
2. tropical
3. Possible answers: hot or warm
4. nervous
5. smog
6. Possible answers: warm or hot
7. arid
8. climate
9. cool
10. snowy

CHAPTER 3 PEOPLE: WHAT DO THEY DO?

Check Your Understanding — p. 23

1. Salespersons
2. Probably all except for food preparation workers and truck drivers
3. Food preparation workers
4. Most general managers and top executives, computer programmers, teachers, computer systems analysts, engineers, lawyers, accountants
5. Answers will vary with experience and understanding. Sample answer: Salespersons, general managers and top executives, teachers, receptionists, nurses, lawyers
6. Truck drivers, nurses

Review   p. 28

1. g.
2. c.
3. h.
4. e.
5. j.
6. i.
7. d.
8. a.
9. f.
10. b.

Test Yourself   p. 29

1. c.
2. b.
3. a.
4. c.
5. c.
6. b.
7. a.
8. b.
9. a.
10. c.

CHAPTER 4 PEOPLE: WHAT'S THIS PERSON LIKE?

Check Your Understanding   p. 33

1. Computer Project Manager
2. Administrative Assistant
3. small, fast-paced
4. SF   San Francisco
   St.   Street
   Admin.   Administration
   pt   part time
   Mac   Macintosh
5. well-organized, efficient, reliable, self-motivated, bright, energetic, flexible, ambitious, talented

Review   p. 40

Answers will vary.

Test Yourself
p. 40

1. Possible answers: efficient, dependable, reliable, responsible
2. intelligent
3. friendly
4. warm
5. Possible answers: dependable, reliable, responsible
6. Possible answers: dependable, reliable, responsible
7. warmth
8. talents
9. generous
10. Possible answers: efficient, dependable, reliable, responsible

CHAPTER 5 FOOD: WHAT DO YOU EAT?

Check Your Understanding
p. 45

1. **a.** the U.S. Department of Agriculture
   b. shouldn't
   c. should
   d. bread, cereal, rice, pasta
   e. are
   f. bread, cereal, rice, pasta
   g. fats, oils, and sugars
   h. low in fat
   i. every day
   j. are
2. sparingly   not very much
   guide   recommendation
   serving   portion
   diet   the food you eat
   poultry   chicken
3. Answers will vary.

Review
p. 53

1. ingredients
2. Possible answers: fruit, vegetables
3. recommends
4. daily
5. energy

Test Yourself   p. 53

1. cereal
2. sugar
3. milk
4. bread
5. pear
6. apple
7. Possible answers: fish, chicken
8. Possible answers: fish, chicken
9. vegetables
10. yogurt

CHAPTER 6 FOOD: WHAT DO YOU DRINK?

Check Your Understanding   p. 58

1. **a.** China
   b. student
   c. people share a teapot
   d. three
   e. formal
   f. a lot
   g. relaxed
   h. oolong
2. Answers will vary.

Review   p. 63

1. S	**6.** D
2. D	**7.** D
3. S	**8.** S
4. D	**9.** D
5. S	**10.** S

Test Yourself   p. 63

1. b.	**6. a.**
2. a.	**7. a.**
3. b.	**8. b.**
4. b.	**9. a.**
5. b.	**10. a.**

Check Your Understanding   p. 68

1. Thursday, 6-7:30 P.M.
2. Monday and Wednesday
3. Stress Management
4. Weight Management
5. Job Search Workshop
6. Team Sports: Volleyball, Basketball
   Exercise Classes: Aerobics, Yoga
   Art Classes: Ceramics
   Dance: Jazz Dance, Ballet
   Martial Arts: Tai Kwan Do
   Health and Stress Management: Stress Management, Weight Management
   Career Management: Job Search Workshop
   Other: Swim Lessons

Word Forms   p. 71

volleyball player
martial artist
swimmer
guitarist
ceramicist, artist
basketball player
singer, vocalist
ballerina, dancer
dancer
weight lifter

Review   p. 76

Answers will vary.

Test Yourself   p. 76

1. b.   6. b.
2. b.   7. c.
3. c.   8. a.
4. c.   9. b.
5. c.   10. b.

Check Your Understanding   p. 82

1. **a.** F
   b. T
   c. T
   d. T
   e. F
   f. T
   g. F
   h. F
   i. T
   j. F

Review   p. 88

Antonyms
top/bottom
opposite/same
win/lose
drop/pick up
challenging/easy
first/last
empty/full
opponent/team member
begin/end

Synonyms
instructions/directions
successive/next

Test Yourself   p. 88

1. players
2. playing pieces
3. 12
4. gameboard
5. squares
6. opposite
7. first
8. begins
9. forward
10. diagonally

Check Your Understanding   p. 94

1. **a.** L: broom; S: needle, string, thumb tack, rubber band, tweezers, tape, knife, scissors, pencil
   b. D: needle, thumbtack, knife, scissors (all are sharp)
   c. E (more tham $10; students may use a different dollar figure): broom
   d. Answers will vary.
   e. Answers will vary.
   f. Answers will vary.

Associated Meanings   p. 98

1. spoon (doesn't turn)
2. rub (doesn't apply force)
3. hold (doesn't involve pulling)
4. splinter (isn't a tool)
5. kitchen (isn't a name for a tool)
6. mirror (doesn't rub)
7. rubber band (isn't an eating tool)
8. open (doesn't require a sharp tool)
9. baby (doesn't use tools)
10. hammer (isn't a kitchen tool)

Review   p. 100

1. hammer-pound
2. tape-attach
3. needle-sew
4. tweezers-pull
5. screwdriver-screw
6. scissors-cut
7. pencil-write
8. spoon-stir
9. towel-dry
10. key-open

Test Yourself   p. 100

Answers will vary. Possible answers:
1. dry off, with a towel
2. cut them, with scissors
3. cut it, with a knife
4. pull it out, with tweezers
5. write it down, with a pencil
6. sew it, with a needle
7. open it, with a key
8. fix it, with a screwdriver
9. attach it, with tape
10. tie them, with string

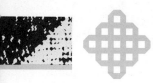

Check Your Understanding   p. 105

1. **a.** monitor
   b. graphic applications/graphics
   c. font
   d. memory
   e. mouse
2. Hardware: monitor, mouse, keyboard
   Software: spreadsheets, word processing, memory, fonts, application, graphics

Review   p. 111

Crossword with answers

		¹m		²e	a	s	y		³f	i	l	e		
⁴t	o	o	l						o					
		u		e			⁵o		n					
		s		⁶c	o	m	p	u	t	e	r			
		e		t			e				⁷t			
	⁸p	e	r	s	o	n	a	⁹l		¹⁰m	o	d	e	m
	a			o				a		e			x	
	d			n		¹¹r	e	p	o	r	t		t	
		¹²d	i	s	¹³k			t		g				
			c		e			o		¹⁴e	¹⁵m	a	¹⁶i	l
					y			p			a		c	
					b						c		o	
¹⁷m	o	n	i	t	o	r			¹⁸i			n	
e				a					b			s		
n			¹⁹p	r	o	g	r	a	m					
u				d										

Test Yourself   p. 112

1. mouse
2. keys
3. personal computer
4. programs
5. multimedia
6. CD-ROMs
7. graphics
8. text
9. software
10. documents

124

Appendix

LIST 1: ALPHABETIZED BY CHAPTER

Chapter 1 Places: Where Are You From?

Africa	Egyptian	Indian	the Middle East
Asia	El Salvador	Iran	North America
Brazil	El Salvadorian	Iranian	Peru
Brazilian	Ethiopia	Italy	Peruvian
Cambodia	Ethiopian	Italian	Poland
Cambodian	Europe	Jamaica	Pole
Canada	Ghana	Jamaican	Romania
Canadian	Ghanaian	Japan	Romanian
the Caribbean	Greece	Japanese	Russia
China	Greek	Korea	Russian
Chinese	Haiti	Korean	Somalia
Dominican	Haitian	Latin America	Somalian
Republic	Hungary	Lebanon	Southeast Asia
Dominican	Hungarian	Lebanese	
Eastern Europe	immigrant	Mexico	
Egypt	India	Mexican	

Chapter 2 Places: How's the Weather?

arid	degree	hot	snow
blue	depressed	humid	strange
breeze	drizzle	ice	sun
Celsius	dry	irritable	temperature
clear	energetic	light	(thunder)storm
climate	Fahrenheit	lightning	tropical
cloud	fog	low pressure	unsettled
cold	forecast	nervous	warm
conditions	front	rain	wet
cool	happy	region	wind
cranky	heavy	sad	
crazy	high pressure	showers	

Chapter 3 People: What Do They Do?

accountant
advise
architect
assign
blueprint
cash register
computer system
computer systems analyst
corporate manager
curriculum

design
draw
electrical engineer
electrical system
elementary school teacher
employment
lawyer
occupation
operate
plan

prepare
profession
project
receptionist
require
responsibility
restaurant cook
salesperson
schedule

Chapter 4 People: What's This Person Like?

ambitious
bright
dependable
efficient
energetic
fast-paced
flexible

friendly
funny
generous
helpful
independent
individual
intelligent

kind
nice
out-going
references
reliable
responsible
salary

self-motivated
sensitive
strong
talented
thoughtful
warm
well-organized

Chapter 5 Food: What Do You Eat?

apple
asparagus
beans
bread
cereal
choices
connection
daily
diet
eggs
energy

fats
fish
flavor
foods
foundation
fresh
fruit
healthy
homemade
ice cream cones
ingredients

maintain
necessities
nutritious
often
pear
pleasures
potato
poultry
recommend
servings
source

sparingly
steak
sugar
tomato
tradition
vegetables
wheat
yogurt

Chapter 6 Food: What Do You Drink?

always	flavor	informal	serve
brew	formal	pours	smells
casual	guests	rare	smooth
common	host	refills	teapot

Chapter 7 Fun: What Do You Like to Do?

advanced	guitar	stress management
aerobics	intermediate	swimming
ballet	jazz dance	tae kwan do
baseball	learn (piano)	take (a class)
basketball	martial arts	team sports
beginning	piano	volleyball
career management	play (a sport)	weight lifting
ceramics	practice (tae kwan do)	weight management
co-ed	resumé writing	workshop
do (yoga)	singing	yoga
fitness	soccer	

Chapter 8 Fun: What Do You Like to Play?

beads	drop	marbles	strategy
begin	first	opponent	successive
block	full	opposite	take turns
bottom	game board	plan	team
buttons	hole	playing pieces	team member
challenging	instructions	remain	top
contain	last	rules	win
cup	lose	skill	
direction	luck	square	

Chapter 9 Tools: Which Do You Need?

absorb
attach
bend
carve
cut
slice
dry
fork
hammer
hit
hold
key
knife
mirror
mix
needle

open
pencil
pierce
pin
poke
pound
pull
reflect
rub
rubber band
scoop
screwdriver
sew
sharpen
shave
spoon

stab
stick
stick
stick
stir
stretch
string
tape
(thumb) tack
tie
towel
turn
twist
wire
wrench
write

Chapter 10 Tools: Can Computers Help You Learn?

application
bundle
button
charts
command
component
desktop
display
document
e-mail
export
file

font
function
graphics
icon
import
integrated software
interactive videodisk
keyboard
laptop
memory
menu
merge

modem
monitor
mouse
multimedia
notebook
personal computer
program
software
spreadsheets
text
tutorial
word processing

LIST 2: ALL WORDS ALPHABETIZED

absorb	Chinese	energetic*
accountant	choices	energy
advanced	clear	Ethiopia
advise	climate	Ethiopian
aerobics	cloud	Europe
Africa	co-ed	export
always	cold	Fahrenheit
ambitious	command	fast-paced
apple	common	fats
application	component	file
architect	computer system	first
arid	computer systems analyst	fish
Asia	conditions	fitness
asparagus	connection	flavor
assign	contain	flexible
attach	cool	fog
ballet	corporate manager	font
baseball	cranky	foods
basketball	crazy	forecast
beads	cup	fork
beans	curriculum	formal
begin	cut	foundation
beginning	daily	fresh
bend	degree	friendly
block	dependable	front
blue	depressed	fruit
blueprint	design	full
bottom	desktop	function
Brazil	diet	funny
Brazilian	direction	game board
bread	display	generous
breeze	do (yoga)	Ghana
brew	document	Ghanaian
bright	Dominican	graphics
bundle	Dominican Republic	Greece
button	draw	Greek
buttons	drizzle	guests
Cambodia	drop	guitar
Cambodian	dry*	Haiti
Canada	e-mail	Haitian
Canadian	Eastern Europe	hammer
career management	efficient	happy
carve	eggs	healthy
cash register	Egypt	heavy
casual	Egyptian	helpful
Celsius	El Salvador	high pressure
ceramics	El Salvadorian	hit
cereal	electrical engineer	hold
challenging	electrical system	hole
charts	elementary school teacher	homemade
China	employment	host

*Appears more than once.

hot
humid
Hungarian
Hungary
ice
ice cream cones
icon
immigrant
import
independent
India
Indian
individual
informal
ingredients
instructions
integrated software
intelligent
interactive videodisk
intermediate
Iran
Iranian
irritable
Italian
Italy
Jamaica
Jamaican
Japan
Japanese
jazz dance
key
keyboard
kind
knife
Korea
Korean
laptop
last
Latin America
lawyer
learn (piano)
Lebanese
Lebanon
light
lightning
lose
low pressure
luck
maintain
marbles
martial arts
memory
menu

merge
Mexican
Mexico
mirror
mix
modem
monitor
mouse
multimedia
necessities
needle
nervous
nice
North America
notebook
nutritious
occupation
often
open
operate
opponent
opposite
out-going
pear
pencil
personal computer
Peru
Peruvian
piano
pierce
pin
plan*
play (a sport)
playing pieces
pleasures
poke
Poland
Pole
potato
poultry
pound
pours
practice (tae kwan do)
prepare
profession
program
project
pull
rain
rare
receptionist
recommend
references

refills
reflect
region
reliable
remain
require
responsibility
responsible
restaurant cook
resumé writing
Romania
Romanian
rub
rubber band
rules
Russia
Russian
sad
salary
salesperson
schedule
scoop
screwdriver
self-motivated
sensitive
serve
servings
sew
sharpen
shave
showers
singing
skill
slice
smells
smooth
snow
soccer
software
Somalia
Somalian
source
Southeast Asia
sparingly
spoon
spreadsheets
square
stab
steak
stick
stir
strange
strategy

*Appears more than once.

stress management
stretch
string
strong
successive
sugar
sun
swimming
tae kwan do
take (a class)
take turns
talented
tape
team
team member
team sports
teapot

temperature
text
the Caribbean
the Middle East
thoughtful
(thumb) tack
(thunder) storm
tie
tomato
top
towel
tradition
tropical
turn
tutorial
twist
unsettled

vegetables
volleyball
weight lifting
weight management
well-organized
wet
wheat
win
wind
wire
word processing
workshop
wrench
write
yoga
yogurt